THE CARNEGIE FOUNDATION FOR THE ADVANCEMENT OF TEACHING

THE COLLEGES AND
THE COURTS

1941-45

Recent Judicial Decisions Regarding
Higher Education in the United States

By M. M. CHAMBERS

Assistant Director, Commission on Implications of
Armed Services Educational Programs,
American Council on Education

WITH A FOREWORD
By EDWARD C. ELLIOTT
President-emeritus, Purdue University

NEW YORK CITY
522 FIFTH AVENUE
1946

This publication was made possible by funds granted by Carnegie Corporation of New York. That corporation is not, however, the author, owner, publisher, or proprietor of this publication, and is not to be understood as approving by virtue of its grant any of the statements made or views expressed herein.

340
C445c
1941·45

D. B. UPDIKE, THE MERRYMOUNT PRESS, BOSTON
PRINTED IN THE UNITED STATES OF AMERICA

Contents

PART FIVE

Financial Support from Private Sources; Institutional Property; Other Matters

FOREWORD

FOR more than a dozen years, Dr. M. M. Chambers, with a distinctive single-mindedness, has cultivated that most important field of educational control represented by the decisions of the higher courts of the states and the nation. The present publication is the result of his latest experienced efforts to make available to administrators and students the judicial interpretations of the past five years relating to higher education. Thus he continues his valuable scholarly service for the clearer comprehension of certain social trends directly affecting American higher education of the present and of the future.

The current records of "education on trial" referred to in the present study would seem to warrant the prediction that educational institutions must anticipate that, more and more, not only their established practices but also their plans for development may be submitted to judicial testing. Each year new stakes are driven, marking new boundaries within which educational institutions will conduct their affairs. These changing boundaries are indicative of the evaluation of educational institutions in an ever-changing society. New precedents provide new obstacles and new opportunities.

During the period of the war, Dr. Chambers served in the Army Air Forces. Immediately following the close of his military service, he indicated a desire to give attention to that subject which for many years had been his professional hobby. It was a great personal satisfaction to give him encouragement. Through the generous interest of the officers of Carnegie Corporation of New York, and of the Carnegie Foundation for the Advancement of Teaching, ways and means were provided for the minimum expenses involved in the assembling and preparation of this material. For Dr. Chambers this has been a labor of love—

a labor that certainly is not without profit to those who would have an understanding of the old and new channels for social action affecting the development and expansion of our education.

EDWARD C. ELLIOTT

June 5, 1946

PREFACE

THIS is the story of some 175 decisions of the higher State and Federal courts in cases affecting universities and colleges in America during the half-decade just past.

It carries forward through that period from the point where the story was dropped in an earlier companion volume, The Colleges and the Courts, 1936–40, a book of 141 pages published by the Carnegie Foundation for the Advancement of Teaching in 1941, which was in turn preceded by The Colleges and the Courts, a 563-page volume by Edward C. Elliott and M. M. Chambers published in 1936 by the same foundation, containing the story of more than a century preceding that year. These two earlier volumes are now out of print, but copies are accessible in all parts of the country in university and public libraries, and in the offices of many college and university presidents.

The contents hereof are arranged in a manner similar to the organization of the two predecessor volumes. A few of the chapters and parts of chapters have appeared previously or concurrently under my name in the following educational journals: The Educational Record (American Council on Education, Washington, D. C.); the Association of American Colleges Bulletin (New York City); the American Association of University Professors Bulletin (Washington, D. C.); the Journal of Higher Education (Ohio State University, Columbus, Ohio); College and University Business (Nation's Schools Publishing Company, Inc., Chicago); and School and Society (Society for the Advancement of Education, Inc., New York City). Acknowledgment is gratefully made to the editors and publishers of these journals for permission to reorganize, revise, and incorporate those materials.

The several units of the National Reporter System were used as the sources of the court reports, and permission to make occasional direct quotations from the opinions of the judges printed therein under copyright was generously granted by the West Publishing Company of St. Paul. University and college presidents and business officers have often supplied me with information by correspondence. Of this I am keenly appreciative. Space forbids explicit mention of all my benefactors.

M. M. CHAMBERS

Washington, D. C.
July 1, 1946

INTRODUCTION
SOME TRENDS OF 1941–45

THE period of World War II exhibited many contrasts with that of its predecessor a generation ago. The first world war brought with it much bitter prejudice against Americans whose national origins were traceable to enemy countries, dealt heavy blows to the teaching of the languages and cultures of adversary belligerents, and gave rise to an unhealthy aftermath revival of racial and religious antagonisms within the United States. World War II was not only more nearly free from those characteristics, but also saw a wave of tolerance toward all "common men," a stimulation of the study of foreign languages, and definite progress toward reduction of onerous discrimination against individuals because of race or religion. These tendencies manifested themselves in the law and practice of higher education in America.

WHO SHALL BE EDUCATED?

Highlights regarding the ever-important right to admission as a student include the United States Circuit Court of Appeals decision in 1945 that the Enoch Pratt Free Library in Baltimore, though managed by a private charitable corporation, cannot exclude a qualified Negro applicant from its library training class solely because of her race. In this instance the library, supported in large part by municipal public funds, is subject to the restraints of the Fourteenth Amendment to the Constitution of the United States in the same manner as are the states and their instrumentalities.

To what extent and how soon the principle may be extended in the field of privately controlled higher education is problematic; but the possibility becomes substantial upon reflection that although only a few private colleges and universities now receive direct appropriations of public money, they almost universally receive the practical equivalent thereof in the form of tax exemptions, and currently in many instances a substantial portion of their income from tuition fees is paid by the national government on behalf of war-veteran students. On broader grounds, it will be remembered that in final analysis the preservation and supervision of educational trusts devolves upon the courts of equity, and the existence of educational corporations is at the sufferance of the state, which may regulate them in the public interest.

New York has a statute forbidding tax-exempt institutions from denying their facilities to any qualified person solely because of race or religion. In 1945 a litigant challenged the continuance of tax exemption on the alleged ground of failure of the state to investigate and determine the fact of non-discrimination —unsuccessfully, but so only because his procedural approach was premature and inadequate to provide a test of the merits in a case of a party allegedly directly aggrieved.

It is also notable that a New Jersey court, required to determine the eligibility of an institution for the privilege of tax exemption, based its negative decision in part upon evidence that the institution discouraged the admission of Negro students, and declared that such a policy was not indicative that a corporation is charitable in operation. These inklings may constitute a "handwriting on the wall" presaging modification of the once widely-accepted doctrine that a tax-exempt privately controlled educational institution may admit or exclude whom it will, without being subject to inquiry as to whether its admission practices bear any proper relation to individual educational rights and capacities.

THE LEGAL POSITION OF STATE AND MUNICIPAL INSTITUTIONS

A most significant occurrence is the inclusion in the completely revised Constitution of Georgia, adopted in 1945, of a section (first adopted as an amendment in 1943) which unequivocally confirms and perpetuates in the hands of the Board of Regents of the University System of Georgia all the powers it possessed at that time, thus definitely establishing it as a constitutionally independent corporation invested with a sphere of authority within which it is coordinate with the state legislature and immune from statutory interference. The event is of especial importance because the board controls all institutions of higher education operated by the state, and is in a position to develop a properly coordinated and inclusive state system.

Moreover, Georgia becomes a new addition to the relatively small number of states wherein the constitutionally independent status of one or more state institutional governing boards has been established and confirmed in the last half-century. The University of Michigan, the Michigan State College of Agriculture and Applied Science, the University of Minnesota, the University of California, the University of Colorado, the University of Idaho, and the Oklahoma Agricultural and Mechanical College have a similar status in their respective states. The Utah Constitution apparently places the University of Utah and the Agricultural College of Utah in the same position, but there seems to have been no occasion on which the state supreme court has made any pronouncement on the subject. The South Dakota Board of Regents of Education, governing all state institutions of higher education, is provided for in the state constitution, but the course of legislation and litigation indicates that its constitutional powers, though interpreted to be substantial and extensive, are somewhat less broad than those established in the other states just mentioned.

An Idaho decision of 1943 reaffirmed the position of the University of Idaho, declaring that a state statute regarding nepotism could not have been applicable to the university even if the legislature had so intended.

The principle that the so-called municipal colleges and universities are in fact agencies of the state, and are not in legal contemplation at all comparable to the various departments of the city government, was announced anew in New York and Michigan decisions.

COLLEGE AND TAX COLLECTOR

In the realm of charter exemptions from taxation, Hamline University in Minnesota and William Jewell College in Missouri succeeded in having their charters interpreted by their respective state supreme courts as validly exempting from state taxation all their property, including lands held as investments.

On the other hand, the supreme court of North Carolina made an exceedingly strict construction both of the Elon College charter and of the constitutional provisions for tax exemption, interpreting both to embrace only the campus and buildings actually in use for educational purposes, and holding that a downtown business building held by the college as an investment with all income applied exclusively to educational uses was taxable under the constitutional requirement that "taxes on property shall be uniform as to each class of property taxed."

Among cases wherein the issue depended upon general statutory exemption clauses, notable was the 1945 decision in Oklahoma regarding the assessment of a farm owned as an investment by Phillips University. The court overruled its own decision of 1930 on the same point, thus overturning a precedent of many years' standing, and announced that in 1946 and thereafter the statutory exemption of educational and charitable institutions would apply only to property owned and physically used by them for their stated purposes.

In the field of federal estate and income taxation, an interesting development was the disposition of certain cases involving the exemption of transfers to charitable corporations devoting a large part of their activities to the advocacy of specific changes in existing law or legislation. In 1941 a divided United States Circuit Court of Appeals held that a bequest to the Methodist

Board of Temperance, Prohibition, and Public Morals was deductible from the testator's estate as exempt from the federal estate tax, notwithstanding the lobbying activities of the legatee organization. The dissenting judge adhered to the English and Massachusetts rule that political agitation or propaganda is not a charitable purpose eligible for tax exemption; but the majority of the court, reflecting that the primary purpose of the organization was religious and charitable, remarked that many charitable corporations necessarily engage in some incidental efforts to obtain the enactment of desired legislation, and that their essential character is not thereby changed.

Two other United States Circuit Court of Appeals decisions of 1945 denied exemption from the estate tax of bequests respectively to an English corporation chiefly engaged in advocating legislation to embody the economic theory of Henry George, and to three trusts established in New York whose principal purposes appeared to be to advocate legislation of three types: to promote labor organization and an economic system of production for use and not for profit, to safeguard and advance civil liberties, and to preserve wilderness conditions in outdoor America. In the last case the United States Supreme Court denied *certiorari* and refused rehearing.

EDUCATIONAL TRUST FUNDS

Decisions on the validity and execution of educational trusts demonstrated anew that a valid voluntary trust is irrevocable, and that courts of equity will direct appropriate modifications of its operation in order to effectuate the charitable intent in a practicable manner, and appoint trustees when necessary to continue the trust. One decision exemplified the principle that an attempt to create a charitable trust is invalid if the projected trust will serve no public benefit. In this same instance, however, a subsequent reinterpretation of the will and codicils of the donor of the property resulted in the conclusion that an earlier intent to dedicate it to public library purposes, superseded by the attempted creation of an invalid museum trust, is now revived—an excellent illustration of the fact that courts will go far in giving precedence to the general charitable intent, as gathered from "the four corners" of the testamentary instrument.

The testing of a so-called "living trust," in which the donor of the fund reserved for his lifetime the right to direct its investment, to receive its entire income, and to revoke the trust, was a highlight of this period. Owing to an uncertainty as to the designation of the ultimate charitable remainderman (a college), the disposition of the fund was brought to the attention of the Ohio supreme court. Of its own motion the court ordered a reargument of the entire question of the validity of the trust, and decided in favor thereof by the narrowly divided vote of four to three. In such a case the line between a valid educational trust and a mere personal agency which dies with its maker presents difficult questions. The strength of the dissent in the Ohio court in this instance may have considerable future significance.

As to the management of institutional endowment funds, it is noteworthy that the investment by Goucher College of a minor fraction of its endowment resources in the erection of income-producing residence halls for students, with arrangements for amortization within the estimated useful life of the buildings, received judicial approval as a prudent practice.

Another case in the same state, however, involving the somewhat tangled affairs of a financially weak denominational college now defunct, illustrated well the dangers of an institution's borrowing its entire endowment fund for investment in financially nonproductive college plant.

RESPONSIBILITY FOR PERSONAL INJURIES

Suits for damages in tort against colleges and universities were unusually numerous, and several of the decisions indicated a continued trend away from the earlier doctrines of immunity, probably presaging further rapid change in this branch of the law.

Mr. Justice Wiley Rutledge, serving on the United States Court of Appeals for the District of Columbia when the case of Georgetown University came up to that tribunal, wrote an extraordinarily comprehensive and lucid exposition of the history and present status of the tort responsibility of charitable corporations. It will be recalled that the lower court had held Georgetown University liable in damages to a private nurse injured while serving a patient in its hospital, on the ground that she was a "stranger to the charity" and therefore not barred from indemnification by being a "recipient of the charity." The six judges sitting in review of the case were unanimous for affirmance of the judgment against the university, but were evenly divided as to the reasoning. Three were satisfied with the doctrine of the lower court; but three, including Justice Rutledge, concurred in his cogent opinion that the decision ought to stand on broader ground. They would abandon the distinction between "strangers" and others, and hold the institution responsible alike to all persons injured by its negligence, in the same manner as other tort-feasors. Their conclusion is that charitable immunity, leaving an innocent injured party without a legal remedy, has no sound basis. Institutions can protect themselves by carrying liability insurance, Mr. Justice Rutledge pointed out; and it is neither necessary nor humane to perpetuate unrealistic and tenuously reasoned legal theories which cannot but result in cases of harsh injustice.

Brigham Young University was also held responsible in damages to a student injured in a laboratory through the alleged negligence of an instructor, by the United States Circuit Court of Appeals; the decision was based in part on a study of the reasoning in Utah state decisions. Manifestly a turning point has been reached in the consideration of tort cases by the federal judiciary, which previously adhered to the theory of charitable immunity.

Among the states, New York, Connecticut, and California exhibit the newer view in cases denying immunity to New York University, Yale University, and Stanford University. As to state-controlled institutions the movement is not so far advanced, but state immunity has been waived in New York, and the State College of Forestry and various state teachers colleges have been held responsible for negligence.

War-Born Litigation

Relatively few cases stemming directly from the circumstances of the national war effort had reached the courts of last resort by the end of 1945, though many of the decisions of the period were more or less subtly affected by the pervasive conditions of wartime, as is always inescapable.

The compatibility of membership on a state institutional governing board with service in the armed forces gave rise to some litigation, but in some instances did not proceed to that stage. The supreme court of Oklahoma determined by a divided decision that a member of the board of regents of the University of Oklahoma vacated his office when he entered upon active duty as an officer in the Army. The dissent indicated the difficulty of the question; and always decisions in such cases must depend upon the precise wording and interpretation of the particular state constitution concerned.

The Wisconsin supreme court sustained the compatibility of the state university presidency with service as civilian head of the national Selective Service System in the pre-war months. The reader of this volume will also encounter one federal court case involving seizure by condemnation of an educational plant for war purposes; and two state court decisions to the effect that the use of institutional property for the training of members of the armed services did not affect its exemption from taxation under state statutes.

It is probable that more cases concerned directly with relations of educational institutions and educational personnel with the war activities of the federal government and the states will reach the higher courts in 1946 and thereafter. No doubt the courts will also be presented with cases related to demobilization and reconversion, concerning such matters as the educational rights of veterans of wartime armed service and of other prospective students, as well as the strenuous readjustments necessary to provide housing and other facilities for a greatly augmented college population.

These prospects assure that the judge-made law of higher education in America will continue to play a crucial role in the orderly progress of advancing human enlightenment and well-being. The truth of H. G. Wells' aphorism, "Civilization is a race between education and catastrophe" comes now to be keenly and widely recognized.

PART ONE

University and College Personnel

CHAPTER I

HIGHER EDUCATION AS A RIGHT

THERE is ample evidence that World War II will be followed by a great and permanent upsurge in college attendance, as was its predecessor a generation ago. During the half-decade 1941–45 the nationwide student work program of the National Youth Administration passed from the scene with the liquidation of that governmental agency. Into the picture came the veterans' education programs provided for in national legislation for the benefit of disabled veterans, and in the broadly conceived act of Congress popularly known as the "G. I. Bill of Rights" under which hundreds of thousands of young men and women returned from service in the armed forces are now receiving limited payments for maintenance and tuition in universities and colleges in all parts of the United States.

The long-standing practice of provision for scholarships and loans for worthy students by private benefactors continues. Judicial decisions affecting one aspect of that beneficent practice are discussed in Chapter III of this volume, entitled Testamentary Trusts for Student Aid.

The present chapter deals with decisions regarding the obligations of divorced parents of children of college age, where such parents are charged with the support and education of their children by court orders.

College Attendance as a "Necessary"

In Oregon a divorced father was ordered to pay his former wife $50 a month for the nurture and education of their 18-year-old daughter until she reached the age of 21 or married, whichever might be sooner; and $25 a month for each of two younger children, to be automatically increased to $50 a month for each for nine months of each year if and when they should go to college. The case reached the state supreme court on an appeal to modify the order, chiefly on the contention that college education was not within the contemplation of the applicable Oregon statute.

The evidence in the record as to the assets and income of the father, whose business was that of buying and selling potatoes, was fragmentary and inconclusive. The mother had decided the daughter ought to go to college, and had reported that the cost at the Oregon State College, exclusive of clothing, laundry, transportation and medical care, was $54 a month. The daughter intended to try to earn a part of her expenses.

On the principle of law involved, the court made an unequivocal pronouncement:[1]

> Whether as necessaries within the contemplation of the common-law rule, or as a provision for education within the purview of our statute, we believe that awards for a college education made in behalf of a child displaying sufficient capacity are permissible. Reason, as well as the public policy of this state, favorable as it is to higher learning, permits no other conclusion.

There was no evidence of the daughter's high-school marks, but the court concluded that sufficient aptitude for college was indicated by the fact that she had completed high school, was willing to earn part of her expenses, and her mother believed she was entitled to go further with her education. The order was modified to reduce the total payment to $75 a month, which would provide the daughter with an estimated residue of $25 a month for college expenses after her mother furnished support for all three children and the local public education of the younger two.

A Pennsylvania court, on a different state of facts, reached a different legal conclusion. Here the divorced father was sole proprietor of a seasonal and fluctuating business of inspecting perishable foods and commodities. The net income had been about $6,700 in 1940, and he had testified that a decline had occurred in 1941. He was paying life insurance premiums aggregating $1,600 a year on policies naming his former wife as beneficiary, and $300 a year expenses on joint property occupied by her. The lower court had ordered him to pay $50 a week for the former wife and a 12-year-old son, and $1,500 a year for the edu-

[1] *Jackman* v. *Short*, 165 Ore. 626, 109 P. 2d 860, 133 A. L. R. 887 (1941).

cation and maintenance of a 19-year-old son at college. On appeal the first part of the order was reduced to $40 a week. As to the son at college, the words of the court were as follows:[2]

> That part of the order of the court below relating to the education and maintenance of appellant's 19-year-old son at college must be vacated. . . . Appellant has been sending his son to the Massachusetts Institute of Technology; and at the hearing before the court below he stated that it was his intention to keep his son there as long as he was able to do so. . . . It is well known that there are worthy parents in all parts of the country, with means greater than this appellant has, who do not furnish their children with the financial assistance necessary for a college education. We cannot say that each has failed in a legal duty to his child and to the state. To hold that the circumstances of this father require him to furnish his son with a college education would be an unwarranted conclusion. Hence in such a matter he is entitled to a measure of discretion, and must be allowed to exercise his own judgment.

In a more recent Michigan case the divorced father was in more affluent circumstances. His average annual income exceeded $10,000. The circuit court ordered him to pay $800 a year for tuition, room and board of his 18-year-old daughter at college, and $25 a month for her support, making a total of $1,100 a year, until she reached the age of 21. The Michigan supreme court, by Justice Boyles with six other Justices concurring, concluded that the need for that amount and the ability of the father to pay were both fully established by the record, and affirmed the decree.[3] Justice Reid alone dissented, pointing out that the daughter's scholastic record was not good enough to meet the admission standards of the University of Michigan, located in her home city, and that no sufficient reason was shown for not attempting to have her admitted to the Michigan State College of Agriculture and Applied Arts, or the Michigan State Normal College, or some other college in Michigan. Her mother wished her to attend Rockford College in Illinois, where the cost for tuition, board and room was $800 a year. She did not want her to go to a coeducational institution, and asserted her belief that attendance at the Michigan State College would be more expensive than at Rockford. The dissenting Justice concluded, however: "The showing as to the necessity and ad-

---

[2] *Commonwealth ex rel. Binney* v. *Binney*, 146 Pa. Super. Ct. 374, 22 A. 2d 598 (1941).
[3] *Titus* v. *Titus*, 311 Mich. 434, 18 N.W. 2d 883 (1945).

visability of the daughter's attending college in the instant case is not highly satisfactory and is somewhat uncertain, but the only means of determining what the result would be is to try out the situation." He thought the order should have recited that if she failed or ceased to attend, the allowance would thereupon automatically cease.

The foregoing three cases, from widely separated states, differ considerably as to the circumstances of the parents, the size of the allowance, and other factors. In general, they indicate continuance of the tendency toward recognition of college education as a right for the children of divorced parents in suitable circumstances. They constitute a significant current in the on-flowing stream of the evolution of educational rights.

CHAPTER II

STUDENTS: ADMISSION; EXPULSION; CREDENTIALS

FURTHER ground has been won in the effort to make higher educational facilities accessible to all qualified persons without distinction as to race, color, or religion.

RACIAL OR RELIGIOUS DISCRIMINATION

An unsuccessful approach to the problem of alleged discrimination in admissions to privately controlled institutions of higher education was recently made in New York, on the basis of a section of the tax exemption statute, dating from 1935, which stipulates: "No educational corporation or association that holds itself out to the public to be nonsectarian and exempt from taxation pursuant to the provisions of this section shall deny the use of its facilities to any person otherwise qualified, by reason of his race, color, or religion."

An application was brought to cancel the tax exemption of Columbia University for the year 1945–46 on the ground that the Tax Commissioner made no inquiry or finding as to whether the university complies with the statute just quoted. The exemption covers real property having an assessed value in excess of $58,000,000, on which the taxes would be about $1,750,000 annually. Construing the statute, the court held that it does not make compliance a condition precedent to exemption, but that it confers upon qualified individuals a right to be not barred from the use of the facilities on account of race or religion. The plaintiff in this case did not claim to be such an individual, and did not allege positively any denial of facilities. Therefore his application to cancel the tax exemption was dismissed.[1]

GRADUATE FACILITIES FOR NEGROES

The young Negro woman who unsuccessfully brought suit in a federal court against the registrar of the University of Missouri for damages for his refusal to admit her to the school of journalism also asked the state courts for a writ of *mandamus* to

[1] *Goldstein v. Mills et al. (Trustees of Columbia University in the City of New York, Intervener)*, 185 Misc. 851, 57 N.Y.S. 2d 810 (1945); affirmed without opinion, 62 N.Y.S. 2d 619 (1946).

compel her admission. The denial of this writ was affirmed by the supreme court of Missouri on the ground that sufficient time must be allowed for the establishment of a course in journalism at Lincoln University (the State institution for Negroes) before the applicant's right matures. Speaking in July 1941 the court said:[2]

> If, upon proper demand, the Lincoln board had refused to establish a course in journalism within a reasonable time, or had informed appellant that it was unable to do so, appellant would have been entitled to admission to that course in the University of Missouri. . . . The present session of the General Assembly will no doubt shortly adjourn. The Lincoln board will then know the amount of funds at its disposal and be in a position to determine whether and when a journalism course can be offered at that school. If, upon proper demand and after a reasonable time, the desired course is not available at Lincoln, appellant will be entitled to take the course at the University of Missouri.

THE ENOCH PRATT FREE LIBRARY TRAINING CLASS

A qualified Negro girl, who was refused admission to the training class for prospective professional employees of the Enoch Pratt Free Library in Baltimore, sought to establish her right to have her application considered without discrimination as to race or color. The federal district court dismissed her suit, but the Circuit Court of Appeals reversed and remanded the judgment, saying: "The plaintiff has been denied a right to which she was entitled."[3]

The Library was founded in 1882 by Enoch Pratt, who erected and furnished a central building at a cost of $225,000, and provided a fund of $833,000, giving both to the city on condition that the city would contribute annually $50,000 for maintenance, including the erection and maintenance of four branches, and that a board of trustees named by him would be incorporated with power to choose their own successors and to manage the Library and make an annual report to the city. Acceptance was effected by a city ordinance, authorized by an act of the state legislature. In 1920 Andrew Carnegie gave the city

[2] *State ex rel. Bluford* v. *Canada, Registrar of University,* 348 Mo. 298, 153 S.W. 2d 12 (1941).

[3] *Kerr et al.* v. *Enoch Pratt Free Library of Baltimore City et al.* (U.S.C.C.A.), 149 F. 2d 212 (1945); reversing (U.S.D.C.), 54 F. Supp. 514 (1944). Certiorari denied, 326 U.S. 721, 66 S. Ct. 29, 90 L. Ed. 36 (1945).

$500,000 for the erection of twenty additional branches, on condition that the city provide the sites and contribute annually at least ten percent of the cost of the buildings for their maintenance. In 1927 a state-authorized city bond issue of $3,000,000 provided additional land and a new building for the central library. The city has greatly exceeded the annual support required as conditions of the Pratt and Carnegie gifts ($100,000), and the total of its appropriations to the library in 1944 was over $850,000. In 1939 the Library employees were covered into the city employees' retirement system.

Since 1928 the Library has maintained the training class for prospective library assistants. Each class is limited to 15 to 20 persons who are allowed to take a competitive entrance examination after being selected on the basis of "initiative, personality, enthusiasm, and serious purpose." Members of the class are paid $50 a month during training, and expected to serve as library assistants at least one year after graduation, if a position is offered. During the existence of the school more than 200 applications had been received from Negroes. All had been rejected. The board of trustees of the Library resolved in 1942: "It is unnecessary and unpracticable to admit colored persons to the Training Class. . . . The trustees being advised that there are colored persons now available with adequate training . . . have given the librarian authority to employ such personnel where vacancies occur in a branch or branches with an established record of preponderant colored use."

The plaintiff in this case, a 27-year-old well-educated Negro girl, alleged violation of the Fourteenth Amendment to the Constitution of the United States, and asked damages under the federal Civil Rights Act, an injunction against further refusal of her application, and a declaratory judgment to establish her right to have it considered without discrimination based on race and color. She was joined by her father, suing as a taxpayer, asking that, if the Library is a private body not bound by constitutional restraints on state action, then the city be enjoined from contributing to it, on the ground that such use of tax funds is *ultra vires*, and violative of the Fourteenth Amendment as a taking of his property without due process of law.

Circuit Judge Morris A. Soper observed that "There can be no doubt that the applicant was excluded from the school because of her race." The principal defense was that the Library is a private corporation and does not perform any public function as a representative of the state. On this the court remarked:

> It is our view that although Pratt furnished the inspiration and the funds initially, the authority of the state was invoked to create the institution and to vest the power of ownership in one instrumentality and the power of management in another, with the injunction upon the former to see to it that the latter faithfully performed its trust. We know of no reason why the state cannot create separate agencies to carry on its work in this manner, and when it does so, they become subject to the constitutional restraints imposed upon the state itself.

Continuing:

> Even if we should lay aside the approval and authority given by the state to the Library at its very beginning, we should find in the present relationship between them so great a degree of control over the activities and existence of the Library on the part of the state that it would be unrealistic to speak of it as a corporation entirely devoid of governmental character. It would be conceded that if the state legislature should now set up and maintain a public library and should entrust its operation to a self-perpetuating board of trustees and authorize it to exclude Negroes from its benefits, the act would be unconstitutional. How then can the well-known policy of the Library, so long continued and now formally expressed in the resolution of the board, be justified as solely the act of a private organization when the state, through the municipality, continues to supply it with the means of existence?

The Supreme Court of the United States has refused to review this decision. Its practical significance may eventually be considerable, in view of the fact that it affords one instance of a private educational corporation being held to be subject to the restraints which the Fourteenth Amendment places upon the states and their instrumentalities.

EXPULSION OF STUDENTS FOR CAUSE

Forfeiture of rights as a student by misconduct is always, of course, a possibility, for it is axiomatic that rights carry with them corresponding obligations. Two students in the Medical College of the University of Tennessee were expelled for selling final examination questions to other students. They sued to compel their reinstatement, alleging that they had not been given a sufficient hearing and had been deprived of the right to make proper defense against false accusations. Specifically, they complained that they had not been given a chance to confront adverse witnesses and cross-examine them. These processes are not required in such a case, decided the Tennessee supreme court, in an opinion in which numerous similar cases in other states were carefully reviewed.

The testimony of the dean of the college and the president of the university was that the stealing and sale of examination questions was of "such momentous import to the good name of the school and of the medical profession generally that it warranted a searching investigation and disciplinary action to the end that the evil complained of be corrected." Accordingly the accused students were first called before a student council consisting of twelve students and the dean, where they denied the charges. The student council, after hearing the evidence against them, recommended to the faculty that they be expelled. The dean then notified them to appear before a faculty committee on a specified day. One of them failed to attend. The faculty committee expelled them. The one who had failed to attend demanded a rehearing. This was granted, and the charges and the testimony were read, and the student was heard in his own behalf. The president of the university was present. Later the president granted an appeal to a committee of the board of trustees of the university. On that occasion the students were present and represented by counsel, and were permitted to testify and introduce witnesses in their own behalf. The committee affirmed their expulsion.

The foregoing procedure was sufficient, for in such cases it is not necessary that the hearing be conducted in strict accordance with all the formalities of a proceeding in a court of law. Conceding that the right to continue one's course in a medical school is a valuable property right, the court pointed out that it is forfeited unless exercised with due regard for the rights of the public.[4] The United States Supreme Court refused to review the decision.

---

[4] *State ex rel. Sherman* v. *Hyman et al.*; *State ex rel. Avakian* v. *Same*, 180 Tenn. 99, 171 S.W. 2d 822 (1942). Certiorari denied, 319 U.S. 748, 63 S. Ct. 1158, 87 L. Ed. 1703 (1943).

ISSUANCE OF TEACHING CREDENTIAL BY COLLEGE

A graduate of the State College of Washington sought a writ of mandate to compel the board of regents of that institution to grant him a life teacher's diploma, on the strength of a statute of 1923 which authorized the board, upon the recommendation of the faculty, to issue life diplomas to candidates who have taught successfully for 24 months and completed at least 12 semester hours in the department of education. He had conducted correspondence on the matter with the dean and the registrar, but no faculty recommendation in his case had been made, and he had at length been informed that no life diplomas would be issued after September 1, 1938. Thereafter he invoked the aid of the courts, but his petition was dismissed because the recommendation of the faculty is an essential prerequisite to the issuing of diplomas by the board of regents.[5]

---

[5] *State ex rel. Brown* v. *Gannon*, 10 Wash. 2d 440, 117 P. 2d 215 (1941).

CHAPTER III
TESTAMENTARY TRUSTS FOR STUDENT AID

IN this day of nation-wide systems of student aid paid from public funds, private philanthropy plays its complementary role, adding much to the variety of the scene. New charitable trusts continue to be created, and the legal principles upon which they are sustained are frequently reinterpreted and developed to apply to varying situations.

Defining the Class of Beneficiaries

Two recent cases illustrate that the creator of a charitable trust may go a long way in defining narrowly the classes of persons eligible for its benefits, without thereby destroying its validity.

An unmarried lady in Indiana, bequeathing her residuary estate to a trust company, directed it to expend the income to further the college education of children of employees of the Pennsylvania Railroad Company living in Fort Wayne. Payments were to be made to only one beneficiary at a time, not to exceed $800 in any year, and for not more than four years to any one recipient. The trust estate actually produced an annual income of about $3,500. Seizing upon this circumstance, a group of collateral heirs contested the will on the ground that the excess income would accumulate unlawfully; and also advanced the argument that the trust was not charitable because it was for the benefit of too small and narrow a class.

In a well-documented opinion the Indiana supreme court concluded that the will created a valid charitable trust. It followed, then, that the disposition of the excess income was subject to determination in accordance with the judicial doctrine of *cy pres*, under which it is the duty of the court of equity having local jurisdiction to modify the administrative provisions in the will, if and when necessary to assure that the benevolent intent is executed in a practicable manner.[1]

A different question as to the designation of the beneficiary class involved the will of a resident of New Jersey who made his

---

[1] *Quinn* v. *People's Trust and Savings Co.*, (Ind.), 60 N.E. 2d 281, 157 A. L. R. 885 (1945).

brother and his two nephews residing in Nassau, Bahama Islands, trustees of his residuary estate for the purpose of providing scholarships for the higher education of deserving children resident in Nassau and in need of such aid. The following sentence was also in the will: "It is my wish that preference in the awarding of these scholarships be always given to the descendants of my brothers and sisters if they are in need of and apply for such assistance."

Relatives attacking the will contended that the quoted sentence made the trust merely a private one for the benefit of members of one family, and therefore invalid as a charity. The court was unimpressed. "A trust for the benefit of the descendants of the donor's relatives would not be a charitable trust; but if a trust be created for a charitable purpose, the giving of a preference to those members of a certain family who come within the general class of beneficiaries does not deprive it of the character of a charitable trust or convert it into a private trust."

The facts indicated that the annual income available would be about $3,000. The court estimated that this would provide four scholarships of $750 each. Only one nephew of the testator was ready for college at the time. "The situation will vary from year to year," said the court, "but it seems likely that the fund will be of real value for the promotion of higher education in the little city of Nassau." A presumption exists that the trustees will administer the trust in a proper manner unless and until the contrary is shown.[2]

DESIGNATION OF THE TRUSTEE

If the purpose of a trust is clear, it is immaterial that no trustee is named, for the court of equity having jurisdiction will appoint a trustee to execute the charitable educational intent. A Kentucky testator bequeathed his residuary estate to his wife for life, and simply stipulated that "at her death it shall remain *hours* in trust to care for *Cemetary* lot and to educate some poor Christian *worthey Girl*." His nieces and nephews contested the will on the ground that the charitable provisions were so indefinite and uncertain as to be unenforceable. The Court sustained the trust, saying: "Certainly there is design, object and purpose

---

[2] *In re Butler's Estate*, 137 N.J. Eq. 48, 42 A. 2d 857 (1945); affirmed without opinion, 137 N.J. Eq. 457, 45 A. 2d 598 (1946).

in the will;" and "No distortion of the plan, wish, or intent is conceivably necessary." The misspelled *"hours"* was obviously a way of expressing a desire to perpetuate the gift as a memorial. Failure to name a trustee was of no consequence at common law, and the contingency is specifically provided for by a Kentucky statute worded as follows:[3]

> No charity shall be defeated for want of a trustee or other person in whom the title may vest; but courts of equity may uphold the charity by appointing trustees, if there be none, or by taking control of the fund or property, and directing its management and settling who is the beneficiary thereof.

A residuary estate of some $90,000 was bequeathed to the University of Notre Dame du Lac, an Illinois corporation, "in memory of my brother, Charles Smith, known in religion as 'Brother Alexander,' who was one of the early associates and workers with Father Sorin, the founder of the University of Notre Dame." The fund was to be designated the "Brother Alexander Memorial Scholarship Fund," to be held and invested by the Board of Lay Trustees of the university, and the net income annually awarded by the president of the university as one or more scholarships "to worthy students of the University of Notre Dame who are preparing for the priesthood in the Congregation of the Holy Cross."

A nephew, next of kin and sole heir-at-law, beneficiary of a specific legacy of between $5,000 and $10,000 value, attacked the will on the ground that the charitable legatee was not in existence at the time of the death of the testator in 1942, and filed a counterclaim alleging the testator had orally contracted with him that in consideration of care by him and his wife, the testator would execute a will giving him his entire estate. Defeated in the lower court, he appealed on the further allegation that it was error to deny a motion to continue the case by reason of his absence with the Army in a foreign country at the time of trial.

It appeared that there was an *Illinois* corporation named University of Notre Dame du Lac in existence continuously since 1934, with office at 120 South La Salle Street, Chicago. It had been in suspension from 1937 to 1944, under an order of dissolution by the Superior Court; but this order was never actually

---

[3] *Young et al.* v. *Redmon's Trustee*, 300 Ky. 418, 189 S.W. 2d 401 (1945).

effective because it had been served only by publication, and it was formally set aside and the corporation restored of record to its standing by a new decree of 1944. Its existence could not be an issue in this case because the existence of a *de facto* corporation cannot be attacked collaterally.

The nephew's rights under the Soldiers' and Sailors' Civil Relief Act of 1940 had not been infringed, because the prosecution of the action would not have been materially affected by his presence or absence at the trial. "Under the statute he was an incompetent witness and could not testify." Moreover, he had estopped himself from asserting his counterclaim by accepting and receipting for part of his legacy under the will without protest or reservation. The applicable words of the court were as follows:

> Testator's intention being that all of the provisions of the will shall take effect, a beneficiary cannot accept that which is given by the will, and set up any right or claim, however legal or well-founded it may have been, which would defeat or prevent a full operation of the will.

Affirming the decision of the lower court which sustained the charity, the Illinois court of appeals concluded a long opinion necessarily wrestling with many technicalities, with a simple and direct statement: "There is no doubt of the intention of this testator."[4]

DISCRETION OF THE TRUSTEE

That the authority delegated to a charitable trustee may be very broad and free from specific restrictions is illustrated by a Tennessee case declaring that the following words in a will created a valid charitable trust: "All the rest and residue of my estate, of whatsoever character and kind and wheresoever situated, real, personal, and mixed, I give, devise, and bequeath to Walter R. Sanders of Nashville, Tennessee, to be used by said Walter R. Sanders for the education of any child or children whom he deems worthy of assistance."[5]

A decision in Iowa hinged upon technicalities concerning the legal identity and continuity of an educational institution. A residuary estate of about $100,000 was left in the hands of a

---

[4] *Continental Illinois National Bank and Trust Company of Chicago* v. *University of Notre Dame du Lac et al.*, 326 Ill. App. 567, 63 N.E. 2d 127 (1945).

[5] *Ratto et al.* v. *Nashville Trust Co. et al.*, 178 Tenn. 457, 159 S.W. 2d 88 (1942).

bank with direction to pay the income in equal parts to Drake University at Des Moines and Penn College at Oskaloosa, to provide annual scholarships of $200 to be awarded by the respective institutions to worthy persons unable to pursue college work without financial assistance. There was to be no discrimination as to sex, creed, or color of the recipients. The will provided that if either institution should cease to exist, the entire income of the trust should go to the surviving institution; and if both should cease to exist, then the trustee was authorized to select some other Iowa institution.

Now in 1933, when Penn College, largely supported by gifts from farmers of the Society of Friends, had encountered heavy financial weather, it had adopted the seemingly necessary and unquestionably legitimate device of setting up a new corporation designated "William Penn College" to rent the plant and operate the college, while the old corporation continued in existence to pay debts, collect delayed gifts, and handle impending mortgage foreclosures. The personnel of the governing boards of the two corporations was identical, and there was no break or interruption in the schedule of the institution. It weathered the financial storm creditably and emerged essentially unchanged except for the alteration of its corporate structure and nomenclature, which was in reality much more a matter of form than of substance. Had Penn College ceased to exist? The court thought not, and indicated that the Oskaloosa institution was entitled to half the income of the scholarship trust.[6]

STUDENT LOAN FUNDS

Examples of valid testamentary trusts for student loans are afforded by cases from Texas, Florida, and California. In the Texas case the words of the will were as follows: "The Trustee shall have power and authority and is hereby directed, out of the income only, if in the judgment of the Trustee the income of the trust is sufficient after the contributions above provided for, to make loans to ambitious and worthy boys and girls, who are financially unable to secure an education and would otherwise be deprived thereof. Such loans shall be in amounts and upon terms

[6] *In re Hagan's Will: Valley Savings Bank* v. *Penn College, et al.*, 234 Ia. 1001, 14 N.W. 2d 638 (1944).

and conditions, and to such boys and girls that may be determined worthy thereof in the discretion of the Trustee, but without regard to residence of the recipients."[7]

The will of a Florida testator specified: "Upon the death or remarriage of my wife, the entire net income derived from said trust estate, or such of it as she may not have disposed of in her will, shall be lent by the surviving trustee to boys and girls who are anxious to obtain an education and because of lack of means, are unable to do so, and as such trustee shall select; such boys and girls to be educated at the Berry School, or such other school or schools as the trustee may select in his discretion." It went on to provide that if recommended by the principal of the school and desired by beneficiary pupil, the loans should be continued to cover expenses of college attendance; and to stipulate that "Notes shall be taken for the amounts furnished, bearing interest at the rate of 5 percent, maturing on or before 5 years from date of finishing the education of such boys and girls, whether in lower school or in college."[8]

A California resident bequeathed her residuary estate to the University of Washington in trust, the income to be used to aid wholly or partially self-supporting girl and women students by gifts or loans as determined by the university authorities. The legal capacity of the university to receive the bequest was challenged, and the adversary parties also argued that no charitable trust was created, because "loans to students could not be said to be charitable." The California court readily took judicial notice of the laws of the state of Washington to observe that the university is authorized to take by will; and disposed of the argument regarding student loans by declaring that by no stretch of the imagination could it be thought that there was any intent to set up a commercial enterprise. Loans, if made, would "permit a larger number to be aided by the bounty of the testatrix, and at the same time encourage the formation of proper habits on the part of the recipients."[9]

---

7 *Powers et al.* v. *First National Bank of Corsicana*, 138 Tex. 604, 161 S.W. 2d 273 (1942).
8 *Pattillo* v. *Glenn et al.*; *Cobb* v. *Same*, (Fla.), 7 So. 2d 328 (1942).
9 *In re Yule's Estate*, 57 Cal. App. 2d 652, 135 P. 2d 386 (1943).

TRUST DEFEATED WHEN THE WILL IS VOID

Though the courts will go far to sustain a charitable trust, it is laboring the obvious to note that all testamentary trusts depend upon the existence of a valid will, executed in accord with the formal requisites as set forth in the statutes and maintained in the common law of the state concerned. A Colorado case affords a curious example of the frustration of a charitable intent by failure in that respect. A husband and wife drafted a joint reciprocal will, providing that upon the death of the surviving spouse the property should go into a permanent trust fund to furnish a scholarship for college education for any boy or girl resident in Denver at least one year, possessing qualifications to excel in study and without sufficient financial resources.

The husband died in 1935 and the instrument was probated as his will, and executed insofar as required until the death of his wife. The wife died in 1942 and the instrument was again offered for probate as her will; but rejected, because the surviving witness who had signed the instrument at the time of its making testified that the wife was not present when he signed, that he could not remember that her signature was on it when he signed, and that he would not recognize her signature if he saw it. In these circumstances, the Colorado supreme court held that the instrument was void as the will of the wife; that she died intestate; and her estate must pass to her heirs, as contended by her administrator.[10]

An attempt was made to save the instrument, if not as a will, then as a contract binding the wife's estate, but this failed, on the court's conclusion that the trust provision, if regarded as a contract, could not have been supported by consideration unless the prior decease of the husband had been foreordained.

[10] *Ireland* v. *Jacobs*, (Colo.), 163 P. 2d 203 (1945).

CHAPTER IV
MEMBERS OF THE FACULTY

CASES involving salaries, tenure, discharge, resignation, and other incidents of the contracts and status of professors and other instructional employees of colleges and universities were unusually numerous during 1941–45. Some of the decisions mark progress toward firmer establishment of a fitting security and dignity for the profession.

BREACH OF CONTRACT BY THE INSTITUTION

Bertrand Russell contracted with the Barnes Foundation at Philadelphia to deliver weekly lectures for five consecutive years, 1941 to 1945 inclusive, at a salary of $8,000 a year. The Foundation dispensed with his services December 31, 1942, three years before the expiration of the contract term. In such circumstances the aggrieved party has a choice of legal remedies, one of which is to sue immediately for damages for anticipatory breach of contract; in this event he is *prima facie* entitled to the full amount of the agreed salary, and the burden of proof is on the defendant to show why the damages should be mitigated, and to what extent. Russell elected this remedy.

The Foundation did not allege any failure on the part of Russell to perform according to the face of the written contract. The only defense was that he had allegedly violated an oral agreement made prior to the signing of the written instrument. This is no defense, because it collides squarely with the well-known "parol evidence rule" to the effect that oral testimony cannot be heard to contradict, vary, or add to the terms of a written instrument which is complete, valid and enforceable on its face. Thus the United States District Court rendered a judgment for Russell on the law of the case, and ordered a trial to determine the amount of damages.[1] An appeal to the United States Circuit Court of Appeals was dismissed because the order appealed from was not a final decision subject to appellate review.[2] At the trial to determine damages Russell was awarded a judgment for $20,000, which was $4,000 less than his agreed salary for the

[1] *Russell* v. *Barnes Foundation*, (U.S.D.C.), 50 F. Supp. 174 (1943).
[2] *Barnes Foundation* v. *Russell*, (U.S.C.C.A.), 136 Fed. 2d 654 (1943).

three years. The $4,000 was adjudged to be a proper mitigation of damages, due to the considerable possibility that a man of Russell's standing would obtain other employment as a teacher before 1946.[3]

Though the original matter in dispute was of no avail as a defense, it may be noted that by the testimony of Russell he understood himself to be bound for less than his full-time services, and free to do other work for pay concurrently; and he had earned from other sources sums exceeding $5,000 during the first two years; while by the testimony of Barnes it had been orally understood that Russell was obligated full-time. The written contract was silent on the point, merely stipulating one lecture a week.

DISCHARGE FOR CAUSE, UNDER TENURE RULES

At Louisiana State University an assistant professor of Romance languages who had been with the university some fifteen years was reappointed in June 1941 for the ensuing academic year, and for an indefinite tenure under the regulations adopted by the governing board in January 1941. On September 9 of that year a complaint was brought to another member of the faculty that the assistant professor had on that date committed acts unbecoming his status. Four days later he appeared before a faculty committee appointed by the president of the university, and received a copy of the written charges against him. He admitted the charges and offered no testimony. Two days later the president notified him that the faculty committee had decided that the charges were of such gravity that he should be discharged; and offered him the opportunity of resigning any time prior to September 20. On September 19 he wrote to the president that he would not resign. Two days later the president wrote him that he was discharged. The discharge was ratified by the governing board of the university at a meeting early in November 1941. Subsequently he sued for reinstatement by *mandamus*, and for recovery of his salary for the academic year. Judgment in the trial court was against him, and was affirmed by the supreme court of Louisiana. The procedure used in effecting his dismissal was held to have been in accord with the tenure regulations.

3 *Russell* v. *Barnes Foundation*, (U.S.D.C.), 52 F. Supp. 827 (1943); affirmed, (U.S. C.C.A.), 143 Fed. 2d 871 (1944); and certiorari denied, 323 U.S. 771, 65 S. Ct. 122, 89 L. Ed. 616 (1944).

There was no merit in his contention that the president was without authority to discharge him, subject to later confirmation by the governing board. The board's proper function is to "review, set aside, or confirm" acts of the president. Normally it meets only four times a year, and obviously the president has authority to manage the institution in the intervals between its meetings.[4]

TENURE APPEAL TO NEW YORK STATE COMMISSIONER OF EDUCATION

A history instructor in Brooklyn College, who had acquired permanent status under the statute of 1940 providing for tenure in the city colleges of New York, was dismissed in June of that year by the Board of Higher Education on the recommendation of a committee which had conducted a hearing and concluded that her "approach to history was static and mechanical and not calculated to integrate the individual background of the student fully with the historical studies pursued under her direction." She appealed to the State Commissioner of Education, whereupon the Board of Higher Education challenged his jurisdiction and took the question of jurisdiction into the courts, where it was held that the public colleges governed by the Board of Higher Education of the City of New York are part of the school system of the state and that the Commissioner of Education has jurisdiction to entertain and determine appeals from decisions of that board in the exercise of its removal power.[5]

REINSTATEMENT AFTER ABORTIVE RESIGNATION

A professor of history and political science at Montana State University who had been with the institution twenty-six years, and who had permanent status under the tenure rules adopted by the state board of education in 1916, was falsely accused of misconduct in 1937 by a young woman who had worked on a WPA historical project under his direction. She, jointly with her brother-in-law, signed an affidavit charging the professor with attempted rape, and placed it in the hands of the president of the

4 *State ex rel. Bourgeois* v. *Board of Supervisors of Louisiana State University and Agricultural and Mechanical College*, 205 La. 177, 17 So. 2d 25 (1944).
5 *Board of Higher Education of the City of New York* v. *Cole*, 176 Misc. 297, 27 N.Y.S. 2d 24 (1941); affirmed, 263 App. Div. 777, 31 N.Y.S. 2d 177 (1941); affirmed, 288 N.Y. 607, 42 N.E. 2d 609 (1942).

university September 27, 1937. Innocent of the charge, but aware of the difficulties involved, the professor discussed the matter with the president and gave him a written resignation dated October 1, 1937. He then employed counsel and sued the brother-in-law for damages for libel and slander, and obtained a judgment in April 1938. Meantime, on December 12, 1937, his accuser made and signed under oath a complete retraction of her charges, in which she said of her affidavit of accusation: "Said written statement is not true. . . . At the time I signed said written statement I was in poor health and did not fully understand and realize the full import of said statement."

On the date of this retraction the professor sent the president a written withdrawal of his resignation. The state board of education had not taken action on the resignation, but was due to meet at the university on the following day. In the morning of the meeting day the professor personally handed the president another written withdrawal of his resignation. The board met, and during the forenoon session, apparently not knowing of the withdrawal, accepted the resignation "in a more or less informal way." At the afternoon session, the professor's counsel personally presented to the board his case for reinstatement, "but nothing came of it."

During the next four years the professor sought reinstatement. The matter was put before the board at eight different meetings. During all that time the vacancy on the faculty continued unfilled. When at length the professor sued for reinstatement by writ of mandate, he won a judgment in the trial court which not only ordered him reinstated, but also included a statement of damages for attorney fees and expenses, and his accrued salary and the manner of payment thereof. The supreme court of Montana affirmed the order of reinstatement, but modified the judgment to exclude the fiscal statement, on the ground that it had not been a part of the pleadings, and under the Montana statute providing for damages in *mandamus* cases the damages are "not those which have arisen out of the prior preclusion or deprivation which the writ itself was invoked in part to redress."

Regarding the resignation and its withdrawal, the court was explicit: "It was as if he [the professor] had delivered the withdrawal to the board itself. It was the duty of Simmons [the president] to call the attention of the board to the withdrawal before it assumed to act on the resignation. Acceptance of the resignation was under the circumstances abortive, the resignation not being legally before the board for action. A tender of resignation is nothing more than an offer to resign," subject to withdrawal at any time until it is accepted by the board.[6]

Settlement of Salary Claim by Accord and Satisfaction

A well-established rule regarding disputed claims for back salary was applied in the case of a teacher at Wilberforce University who sued for a balance of some $995 alleged to be due him for services over the period from 1930 to 1939. The amount claimed represented chiefly a deduction of 10 percent from his salary to which he averred he had never consented. In part it also consisted of charges against him for board and for other items, including "gifts to the football training table" which he disputed. The university had no formal evidence of his acquiescence in the reduction, but was able to show that at times it had given him checks for the amount of the 10 percent cut and that he had indorsed these to the university as gifts. Futhermore, at the end of his period of service he had accepted a check for $162 marked "payment in full for services to date," but had scratched off that notation and made that fact known to the treasurer of the university before cashing it.

On the basis of these facts he obtained a judgment in the trial court, but this was reversed by the court of appeals, which stated the law of the case thus:

> Here, the payee elected to present this check, and he must be held to have collected it upon the terms under which it was tendered; namely, full settlement of his disputed, unliquidated claim. The payee cannot accept the benefit of the check and refuse the condition under which it was tendered, unless the payer has waived this condition and permitted it to be paid as a credit on account and not in full settlement thereof.

Hence the claim was held to have been fully settled by accord and satisfaction.[7]

---

6 *State ex rel. Phillips* v. *Ford et al.*, (Mont.), 151 P. 2d 171 (1944).
7 *Kiser* v. *Wilberforce University*, (Ohio App.), 35 N.E. 2d 771 (1941).

SALARIES IN NEW YORK CITY COLLEGES

A teacher at the College of the City of New York was employed and reemployed annually as a "temporary instructor" successively from 1929 to 1938, when he was appointed an instructor on indefinite tenure. His pay was $2,940 per year from 1932 to 1942, when it was jumped to $4,404. If he had been paid according to the schedule for instructors as set forth in the state Education Law, with annual increments, he would have reached $4,500 by 1940. He sued the Board of Higher Education for the accumulated difference, and won his case, except that his claims for any years prior to 1935 were barred by the statute of limitations. The board's defense was that he had accepted the appointments as "temporary instructor" knowing that he would get no increments under them; but the court was unimpressed, saying: "The difficulty with defendant's contention is that there is no position of temporary instructor provided for in the schedules. There is only one kind of instructor mentioned. . . . It is true that plaintiff agreed to appointment as temporary instructor, but as there is no such position and never was, this agreement is without significance."

This decision was subsequently reversed by a three to two vote of the Appellate Division, but eventually affirmed by the Court of Appeals, which summarized the issue as follows:[8]

> It appears conclusively . . . that the plaintiff was in 1929 appointed in the scheduled position of Instructor for the academic year beginning September 1, 1929, and that his appointment to the same position was renewed from year to year thereafter until he was given permanent tenure. The provisions of Section 889 of the Education Law . . . that compensation and salaries "shall be not less than the salaries and salary increments fixed by the schedules and schedule conditions . . . on file in the office of the State Commissioner of Education on the fifth day of March, 1931" apply to persons holding such positions by successive appointments for single scholastic years without right of permanent tenure, as well as to persons enjoying permanent tenure.

Another case involved certain instructors who petitioned for an order to compel the Board of Higher Education to pay their

---

[8] *Dexter* v. *Board of Higher Education of the City of New York*, 293 N.Y. 39, 55 N.E. 2d 857 (1944); reversing *Same*, 267 App. Div. 189, 45 N.Y.S. 2d 264; and affirming *Same*, 42 N.Y.S. 2d 905 (1944).

salaries according to the schedule adopted December 15, 1927 (providing for automatic increases except when the instructor's services were unsatisfactory) and in disregard of an amendment adopted by the board June 26, 1935 (making any increases beyond the fifth increment conditional upon possession of the Ph.D. degree). Here again the instructors won their case at all stages, and obtained an affirmance by the highest court of the state, the New York Court of Appeals.[9] The board contended that it had reserved the right to amend the schedules of 1927; that the plaintiffs had failed to protest for six years; and that the position of instructor was new after 1935. These arguments were of no avail because the schedules of 1927 had been established as minima in the state Education Law prior to 1935.

A third and similar case was brought by an associate librarian who asked for a declaratory judgment to make void the amended schedule of 1935, and also a bylaw of July 6, 1939 which purported to abolish increments for associate librarians save in exceptional cases; and an order to pay him the difference between what he had actually received and what he would have received under the schedules of 1927. His recovery for 1940 and 1941 was allowed on the basis of "the right to sue to recover a salary definitely fixed by statute." He also recovered for the earlier years, despite the board's contention that retroactive recovery could not be had because he had accepted his pay and signed the payrolls without protest. A city ordinance so provides; but that ordinance applies only to employees of the city, decided the court. "That the Board of Higher Education is an entity separate and distinct from the municipality and is a state agency . . . is now well settled."[10]

LEGAL RELATIONS OF STATE UNIVERSITIES TO THE STATE

For many years the annual budgets of the University of Illinois have carried an item for the salary of an individual designated "Professor and University Counsel." For several recent years this item had been $9,000, the incumbent of the position being the noted jurist, Sveinbjorn Johnson. After 1941 there was

---

[9] *Adams et al.* v. *Board of Higher Education of the City of New York,* 288 N.Y. 652, 42 N.E. 2d 745 (1942).
[10] *Nelson* v. *Board of Higher Education of the City of New York,* 263 App. Div. 144, 31 N.Y.S. 2d 825 (1941), affirmed without opinion in 288 N.Y. 649, 42 N.E. 2d 744 (1942).

an additional item of $900 for another individual as part-time assistant counsel, who also received $2,100 as assistant manager of student loans. Early in 1942 the state attorney general asserted to the board of trustees of the university that he had the legal right to appoint the university counsel. When the board rebuffed him, he wrote to Johnson, purporting to "accept his resignation," which had not been tendered; and at the same time instructed the Auditor of Public Accounts not to issue salary warrants to Johnson and the assistant university counsel. The board subsequently sued for a writ of *mandamus* to compel the Auditor to issue the warrants. The writ was denied on the seemingly narrow technical ground that no specific authority for payment of "Counsel" appeared in the itemized state appropriation act for the biennium; and the board of trustees can make no expenditure except out of a fund duly appropriated for the purpose. Long-standing practice to the contrary, said the court, cannot affect this conclusion.

After this extremely strict disposition of the fiscal aspect of the case, the court went on to discuss the broader issue as to where authority to choose the university's legal counsel resides. It held that the university is a public corporation having a legal personality of its own, and is not required to use the attorney general as its sole legal representative. Consequently it issued a writ to compel the attorney general to withdraw from a current Cook County case in which he had attempted to substitute himself for Judge Johnson as university counsel.[11]

The markedly more independent status of the University of Idaho was expounded by the supreme court of that state in the course of its opinion affirming a judgment in favor of a university nurse who sued for her accrued salary, which had been withheld because she was the niece of the wife of a member of the board of regents who had taken office some years after the original appointment of the nurse. The issues, thought the court, were two: (1) Was the state statute forbidding nepotism intended to be applicable to the university? (2) If so, did the legislature have power to make it so applicable? Both were decided in the negative. The four judges participating agreed in the result, but were divided as to the reasoning, with Justice Ailshie and

---

[11] *People ex rel. Board of Trustees of University of Illinois* v. *Barrett*, 382 Ill. 321, 46 N.E. 2d 951 (1943).

Chief Justice Holden emphasizing that the board of regents is a constitutionally independent corporation. "Its rights, powers, franchises and endowments were placed definitely and permanently beyond the power of the legislature to disturb, limit, or interfere with them" by the Constitution of 1889, which expressly perpetuated them as previously set forth in the Territorial charter of the university. In addition to Idaho decisions on the point, the classic cases in Michigan and Minnesota on the constitutional independence of the state universities were cited and quoted.[12] Justices Givens and Dunlap concurred specially, believing the result could have been reached without discussion of the constitutional aspects.

In Ohio the question of the compatibility of a state university professorship with membership in a city council arose. The General Code of Ohio applicable to municipalities stipulates: "Each member of council shall be an elector of the city, [and] shall not hold any other public office or employment, except that of notary public or member of the state militia, . . ." and declares that a councilman not complying with these requirements shall forthwith forfeit the office. Two members of the faculty of Kent State University, the registrar and the professor of biology, were duly elected to the council of the city of Kent in November 1939, and took office January 1, 1940. When a *quo warranto* action was brought to determine the right to these two council seats, the court concluded that the professors could not have qualified as councilmen except by resigning their public employment at the university. Therefore the seats to which they had been elected were properly filled by appointment by the mayor, in accordance with the statute governing the filling of vacancies.[13]

---

[12] *Dreps* v. *Board of Regents of University of Idaho*, (Ida.), 139 P. 2d 467 (1943).
[13] *State ex rel. Tilden* v. *Harbourt et al.*, 70 Ohio App. 417, 46 N.E. 2d 435 (1940).

CHAPTER V

THE PRESIDENT OF THE INSTITUTION

THE period of World War II saw at least half a dozen litigated controversies concerning university presidents adjudicated in the higher courts. The facts and the judicial opinions clarify somewhat the position of the president, and yield some clues to improved legislation and administration for higher education.

THE STATE UNIVERSITY PRESIDENT IN A FEDERAL JOB

When Clarence A. Dykstra, president of the University of Wisconsin, accepted appointment as Administrator of the National Selective Training and Service Act of 1940, he did so with the concurrence of the board of regents of the university, and with the understanding that he would pay the university the amount of his federal salary less expenses, and continue to draw his regular pay as president of the university. Thereafter the state treasurer refused to honor warrants for the president's salary until he was compelled to do so by *mandamus*. The clause of the Wisconsin constitution on which he relied declares: "No member of Congress, nor any person holding any office of profit or trust under the United States (postmasters excepted) . . . shall be eligible to any office of trust, profit or honor in this state."

The supreme court of Wisconsin held that the president of the state university is a public employee, but not a public officer of the state. Examination of the pertinent statutes showed that all the president's acts of authority are subject to approval by the board of regents, and that the board may remove him at any time without stating specific cause. Noting the apparent disparity between the statutory definition of the president's position and powers on the one hand, and his actual influence and prestige on the other, the court remarked: "Despite these limitations he is in fact the executive and directing head of the institution. The position is one of great power and influence because as a rule it is filled by men highly trained and very able." The board of regents is the legal repository of responsibility and authority for the university; and the president, being an employee of the board with all his acts and even his tenure subject to its will, is not a public officer of the state within the meaning of the constitution. Hence his holding a federal office was not constitutionally incompatible with his position.[1]

SALARIES IN KENTUCKY STATE INSTITUTIONS

Section 246 of the constitution of Kentucky stipulates that "No public officer, except the governor, shall receive more than five thousand dollars per annum as compensation for official services. . . . " In a suit to determine whether this section was applicable to the president of the University of Kentucky and certain professors at the same institution and the president of the Murray State Teachers College, the highest court of the state held that these persons were public employees, not public officers; but were nevertheless within the meaning of the section, because "the public treasury would not be protected by limiting the salaries paid to the few officers of the state unless the salaries of the many employees were likewise limited . . . the word 'officers' must be construed to include, by inference, employees subordinate thereto."

Justice Rees entered a vigorous dissent:

> The president and professors of the University of Kentucky and other state-supported schools are not officers within the meaning of the section, and its limitations should not be applied to them. . . . Today states and their subdivisions engage in manifold activities of which the most far-sighted statesmen of fifty years ago had not the slightest conception. . . . They intended the section to apply to public officers performing official duties, and we should not declare at this late day for the first time that it was intended to include employees. In construing a constitutional provision courts are limited to the language used and are controlled by what the framers of the instrument said and not by what they might have meant to say. . . . I think Section 246 should be construed to mean exactly what it says, and should not be extended beyond the clear implication of the language employed.

The majority of the court, having gone to some length to distinguish independent contractors from officers or employees of the state, concluded that certain attorneys employed on a contingent fee basis in the assessment and collection of delinquent taxes, as well as a technical adviser on public utility rates, were

---

[1] *Martin, Attorney General, v. Smith, State Treasurer*, 239 Wis. 314, 1 N.W. 2d 163 (1941).

not within the meaning of the section because they were independent contractors responsible only for results and not subject to detailed administrative direction. In contrast, the university president and professors were subject to the direction of the governing board as to the manner of their performance.[2]

The impracticability of limiting a state university president's salary, or those of the principal professors, to $5,000 a year, has compelled the exercise of ingenuity to find some means of lawfully providing appropriate compensation. For a time that portion of salaries in excess of $5,000 was paid from the earnings of the Haggin Trust, a private donation to the University of Kentucky with income expendable at the discretion of the board of trustees. More recently the necessary amounts have been given to the university annually by the Keeneland Association, a private non-profit corporation.

AUTHORITY OF BOARD TO ACT REGARDING PRESIDENT

When the president of the Rhode Island State College had reason to believe that he might not be reappointed at the expiration of his current term, or that he might be sooner discharged, he sought relief in the form of injunction to restrain the governing board from "any official action with reference to the college as far as it may affect complainant, from interfering with him as president of the college and with his office and home, and from uttering defamatory statements about him in his capacity as president." He alleged that two of the seven members of the board were disqualified by reason of concurrent holding of other public offices, as prohibited in the statutes.

The board answered with a demurrer, which was sustained by the state supreme court, and the case was dismissed without trial because the complaint was adjudged defective and insufficient. "For aught that appears, it may be that his appointment has expired, or that he was appointed originally to serve at the pleasure of the board, or that he was not duly and legally appointed. A specific allegation of the nature and terms of his employment, whether by appointment to an office or by private contract, which must necessarily be within his knowledge, would reasonably be expected of the complainant in order to enable the

---

[2] *Talbott, Commissioner of Finance,* v. *Public Service Commissioner et al.,* 291 Ky. 109, 163 S.W. 2d 33 (1942).

respondent board to make proper answer." As to the alleged disqualifications of two members of the board, it was held that this was not subject to collateral inquiry and attack. Presumably it could be questioned only in a separate action in *quo warranto*. Thus on account of the lack of pleadings sufficiently complete to reach the legal issues concerned, the record of the case affords no exposition or determination of the issues.[3]

Privileged Communications of the President

The University of Oklahoma medical school librarian was dismissed by the board of regents, whereupon she brought an action in damages for conspiracy against the president of the university and the dean of the medical school. She alleged that the defendants had conspired to secure her discharge, after she had served in the position seven years, by falsely informing the board that she had procured her appointment by misrepresenting her professional training and credentials. The defendants answered with a demurrer, contending that statements made to the board of regents were absolutely privileged. This view was sustained in the trial court and in the state supreme court on appeal: "The statements being absolutely privileged, it is immaterial as to whether they were made with improper motives or whether they were false. . . . Here the alleged slanderous statements were made at a session of the Board of Regents. . . . It has the final word in the employment or discharge of its faculty members and employees. . . . The Board must depend largely upon the President, deans, and department heads for correct information as to the fitness and qualifications of those on the payroll and those seeking employment. . . . The rule of absolute privilege in such a case is for the protection of the public and not for the protection of the officers."[4]

A somewhat similar and nearly contemporaneous case had arisen in the same state when the president of the Colored Agricultural and Normal University of Oklahoma at Langston was sued for slander by a former matron of one of the university dormitories. The president had told the board of regents at a regular session that he had been informed by a police officer that the

---

[3] *Bressler* v. *Board of Trustees of State Colleges*, (R.I.), 21 A. 2d 559 (1941).
[4] *Hughes* v. *Bizzell et al.*, 189 Okla. 472, 117 P. 2d 763 (1941).

matron had been arrested in Guthrie and charged with the crime of immoral conduct, committed with another employee of the university (the superintendent of buildings and grounds). The record showed that the board had previously instructed the president to report "any misconduct or irregularity on the part of any teacher or employee of the university." The supreme court held that the president had acted in the proper discharge of an official duty as defined in the Oklahoma statute covering privileged communications, and "absolute privilege attended the communication which he there made." Accordingly a judgment for the plaintiff in the trial court was reversed and remanded with direction to dismiss.[5] Two of the justices dissented.

RIGHTS OF LOCAL PROPERTY-OWNER AS AGAINST THE PRESIDENT

A rare case having unique aspects arose out of a peculiar local situation at Wilberforce University in Ohio, where a privately owned building and lot, 30 by 150 feet in dimensions, was entirely surrounded by the campus, and was in close proximity to the main entrance, the administration building, the library, dormitories, and other buildings of the university. The owner of the property complained that up to 1936 he had rented his building to a restaurateur, but for four years thereafter had been unable to rent it at all because the president of Wilberforce University maintained a standing threat to dismiss any student who patronized the place. He prayed for injunctive relief, and the trial court granted a permanent order enjoining the president from "interfering in any way with plaintiff in the rental or use of the property . . . so long as the person occupying the same is of good moral character and so long as no acts are permitted to take place therein that would in any way tend to lower the morals of any student of Wilberforce University." This was affirmed by the Court of Appeals, with the comment that it "does not prohibit any proper administrative rule or regulation affecting the conduct of students of Wilberforce University which is uniform in operation and is not directed especially against the plaintiff in the conduct of any business that may be established in the property described."[6]

5 *Sanford* v. *Howard*, 185 Okla. 660, 95 P. 2d 644 (1939).
6 *McGinnis* v. *Walker*, (Ohio App.), 40 N.E. 2d 488 (1941).

The injunction was against the president personally and individually, and not against him in his official capacity or against the board of trustees. Apparently the court had reason to believe the plaintiff was entitled to relief from a species of anticipatory threat deriving from personal animus and not from the university authorities acting officially; and was careful to disclaim any interference with the lawful rule-making power of the University.

AUTHORITY OF THE PRESIDENT AS FISCAL AGENT

Just prior to the exposure of his criminal activities, J. M. Smith, president of Louisiana State University, confected a spurious resolution of the governing board purporting to authorize him to borrow $100,000 on behalf of the university, and took it to the Hibernia National Bank in New Orleans. The bank gave him a cashier's check for that amount payable to the university. He took the check to the National Bank of Commerce in the same city, where the university had had certain deposits for some two years, and obtained that bank's stamp as guarantor of his own personal indorsement thereon. The check was then transmitted through the clearing-house to the Hibernia Bank, which thereupon paid the amount to the Bank of Commerce, where it was deposited to the credit of the university. Smith immediately withdrew the sum by means of a cashier's check payable to a brokerage firm, and gave it to that firm in satisfaction of his personal indebtedness arising out of some concealed and ill-starred speculations in wheat. Within a few days he left the state, and when the transaction became known to the university authorities, they promptly denied any prior knowledge of it, and expressly disavowed any claim to the sum involved. Since a bank deposit made without the knowledge of the one to whom it is credited is not effective until he becomes aware of it and accepts it, the university was completely clear of the matter, never having been a party to it; and the only controversy was between the two banks as to which must sustain the loss. The Bank of Commerce, by reason of its guaranty of Smith's indorsement of the check, stood to lose; and a judgment was rendered for the full amount in favor of the Hibernia Bank.

There was proof that the university governing board had not authorized Smith to perform the transaction or any part of it;

though there was evidence that on certain occasions the board had actually authorized him specially to borrow other specific sums under specified conditions. The main point is that as president he was without general authority to sign checks or notes binding the university by his own signature alone; and the fact that he had on some occasions received carefully defined special authorization only served to strengthen that premise.[7]

The foregoing cases serve to put some fresh paint on the signposts along the boundaries of the status and powers of the state university president. Within the scope of the authority and persuasion of these decisions, (1) he is not an officer of the state, but a public employee under contract with the university governing board; (2) his communications to his governing board related to the discharge of his official duties are absolutely privileged, and thus cannot be made the basis of a suit against him for libel, slander, or conspiracy; and (3) general authority to bind the university by his own signature on checks or notes is not inherent in his position.

---

[7] *Hibernia National Bank in New Orleans* v. *National Bank of Commerce in New Orleans*, 204 La. 777, 16 So. 2d 352 (1943).

CHAPTER VI
MEMBERS OF THE GOVERNING BOARD

DURING 1941–45 two decisions were made as to the right of rival claimants to a seat on a state university governing board. In both cases the issue was the compatibility of board membership with other public offices.

State Senator Ineligible in Michigan

The Regents of the University of Michigan are elected by vote of the people. In April 1941, one Burhans was elected. At the time of the election he was a member of the state senate, and continued as such. His right to a seat on the board of regents was challenged in a *quo warranto* action brought by the candidate who received the next highest number of votes at the same election. The supreme court was unanimous in the conclusion that Article 5, section 7 of the Michigan constitution made void every vote cast for Burhans; but as to the disposition of the vacancy the court was divided. Six of the judges held that the decision in this case created a vacancy to be filled by appointment by the governor as provided in Article 11, section 3 of the constitution.[1]

Three more of the judges concurred specially in this result; but a minority of two consisting of Chief Justice Chandler and Justice Starr dissented, with what seems to be better reasoning. They argued that the present decision created no vacancy, because the vacancy, if such it was, had existed ever since the petitioner in this case, having been duly elected by receiving the second highest number of votes, did not take office; and the court should declare him the rightful regent. Such would have been fully in accord with the statutes and decisions touching *quo warranto* actions.

Service as Army Officer

The compatibility of temporary wartime active duty as an officer in the armed services with various state and local public offices has been litigated in many states with conflicting results.

---

1 *Attorney General ex rel. Cook* v. *Burhans*, 304 Mich. 108, 7 N.W. 2d 370 (1942).

Hence the decision regarding a member of the board of regents of the University of Oklahoma should be understood to be only an example, not necessarily typical of the law or the practice in other states. Its weight is also greatly reduced by the fact that it was a five to four decision.

A member appointed to the board of regents in March 1942 for a seven-year term was ordered to active duty as a reserve officer in the Army in June 1942. Soon thereafter the governor appointed a successor and installed him. The regent on active duty with the Army did not submit a resignation until June 1943, when a new governor promptly accepted it and appointed a new successor. The contest was between the two men appointed successors to the same prior incumbent, by different governors. Five of the judges decided that the office was automatically vacated when the incumbent went on active duty with the Army. Hence the first appointed successor was the rightful holder of the office.[2]

The four dissenting judges maintained that no vacancy occurred until the resignation was accepted; the regent-Army officer was a *de facto* regent until he resigned, even if ineligible from the time when he went on active duty. Two of the same judges added a separate dissent, contending with much force that temporary military service in time of war should not be within the constitutional prohibition of holding "any other office of trust or profit," especially when the commissioned officer is not of the permanent Regular Army; and pointing out that there is no incompatibility at common law.

A Judge as Member of the Governing Board of a Private College

The proprietor of the "Candyland Café" in a Pennsylvania town was tried and convicted for selling liquor to minors, and the state liquor control board revoked his restaurant liquor license. He appealed to the Court of Quarter Sessions, and the revocation order was affirmed. He then appealed to the Superior Court, asking for disqualification of the president judge of the Quarter Sessions, because the minors to whom liquor was sold were students at Westminster College, of which the judge

---

[2] *Wimberly* v. *Deacon*, 195 Okla. 561, 144 P. 2d 447 (1944).

was a member of the board of trustees. Dismissing the appeal, the court said:[3]

> A judge, on assuming office, is not required nor expected to resign, or refuse to accept, membership on the governing bodies of religious, charitable, or educational institutions. Like other men he may perform such civic duties as specially interest him. His membership on the board of trustees of a college will disqualify him from sitting in a case the outcome of which will affect its financial affairs, but this disqualification does not extend so as to prevent his participation in the trial of a case which is concerned with the private and individual affairs of the students of the college, whether as litigants or as witnesses, and whether the case be a civil or a criminal one.

[3] *Appeal of Askounes,* 144 Pa. Super. Ct. 293, 19 A. 2d 846 (1941).

PART TWO

State and Municipal Institutions

. .

CHAPTER VII
THE SPHERE OF
STATE AND MUNICIPAL INSTITUTIONS
IN THE STATE GOVERNMENT

CASES in this category are relatively few, but important, and they deserve more attention than they commonly receive.

CONSTITUTIONALLY INDEPENDENT STATE UNIVERSITY

The fact that the University of Idaho is a constitutionally independent corporation, possessing a wide sphere of authority within which the state legislature cannot interfere, was reaffirmed. Thus the state supreme court held not only that an act of the legislature forbidding nepotism in state employment was not intended to apply to the university, but also that the legislature was without power to make it so applicable, even if it had so intended.[1]

This gives Idaho a renewed warrant for inclusion among the minority of the states, notably Michigan, Minnesota, California, Utah, and Colorado, whose state universities are consistently held to be independent arms of the state government, coordinate with the legislative, executive, and judicial branches.

BOARD OF REGENTS OF UNIVERSITY SYSTEM OF GEORGIA BECOMES CONSTITUTIONALLY INDEPENDENT CORPORATION

An amendment to the Constitution of Georgia, proposed and adopted in 1943, and saved in the comprehensive constitutional revision of 1945, now stands as Article VIII, Section IV:

There shall be a Board of Regents of the University System of Georgia, and the government, control, and management of the University System of Georgia and all of its institutions in said system shall be vested in said Board. . . .

[1] *Dreps* v. *Board of Regents of University of Idaho*, (Ida.), 139 P. 2d 467 (1943).

The said Board of Regents of the University System of Georgia shall have the powers and duties as provided by law existing at the time of the adoption of this Constitution, together with such further powers and duties as may be hereafter provided by law.

The wording of this section leaves no room for doubt of the intent to confirm and perpetuate all the substantial powers possessed by the Board, and to place those powers beyond the ability of the legislature to diminish or impair. Thus clearly Georgia joins the group of states in which the university governing boards have a constitutionally independent status; and the Georgia Board of Regents governs all state-supported institutions of higher education in the state—a situation favorable to the development of a well-coordinated state system.

CONTROL BY STATE LEGISLATURE: ITEMIZING OF APPROPRIATIONS

In a majority of the states the state universities are held to be subject to almost unlimited control by the state legislatures, but in practice the extent and degree of such control varies widely among the states. One example of a strict form of control, the wisdom of which is questionable, is the requirement or custom of extremely detailed itemization of the state appropriations to the institution. This tends to rigidify the institutional planning almost to the point of paralysis, and evidences either an intended or inadvertent lack of confidence in the discretion of the governing board. An example of strict control strictly interpreted is afforded by Illinois, where the supreme court declined to order payment of the salary of the eminent jurist who had long served in a dual capacity as professor of law and university counsel, because there was no specific item for "counsel" in the current appropriation act. The court was unimpressed by decades of custom to the contrary, and also unmoved by the fact that the current salary was being withheld as a result of a litigated controversy between the university and the attorney general, in which the court itself adjudged that the attorney general was in the wrong, as will appear in a later section of this chapter.[2]

In refreshing contrast is a Kentucky opinion sustaining a lump appropriation of $200,000 for capital outlay at the Uni-

[2] *People ex rel. Board of Trustees of University of Illinois* v. *Barrett*, 382 Ill. 321, 46 N.E. 2d 951 (1943).

versity of Kentucky. The appropriation had been attacked on the ground that it was not sufficiently specific to be valid under the constitutional provision that "no money shall be drawn from the state treasury, except in pursuance of appropriations made by law"; and the lower court had held it invalid. The Court of Appeals reversed this part of the decision and enunciated its reason in ringing words:[3]

> The affairs of the University of Kentucky are conducted by a board of trustees in whom the Legislature has vested the duty and authority to operate the University and its properties. This authority necessarily carries with it all the authority, in the exercise of a reasonable discretion, to determine the needs and requirements of the University, and to make the necessary expenditures.

CONTROL OF STATE UNIVERSITY PRINTING

A questionable form of state control is that which forbids a university either to operate presses or to contract for printing, and requires all such work to be requisitioned from a state purchasing officer or so-called "state printer" who lets contracts.

In Wisconsin a taxpayer's suit to enjoin the secretary of state from approving vouchers of the University of Wisconsin for salaries of printers and for purchases of supplies to operate two printing presses was successful, because the statutes currently in force required that all state printing be procured by the state printer on order of the state director of purchases. A section of the state constitution requires contracts to be let to the lowest bidder. The court refused to consider whether the constitution actually prohibits any printing by any state agency, and based its decision solely on the absence of any statute affirmatively authorizing printing by the university. It waved aside the argument that the presses in question, used respectively in the Extension Division and the College of Agriculture, were used for work supported in part by federal funds, and that printing was essential to the efficient conduct of that work. As to that: "If the statutes do not permit administration in the most convenient and economic or effective way, the administrative agencies must secure statutory authorization before administering it in any other way."[4]

---

[3] *Commonwealth ex rel. Meredith* v. *Johnson et al.*, 292 Ky. 288, 166 S.W. 2d 409 (1942).
[4] *Democrat Printing Co.* v. *Zimmerman*, 245 Wis. 406, 14 N.W. 2d 428 (1944).

When it is observed that the taxpayer allegedly aggrieved in this case was a printing company, doubt may well arise that the interests of the people of Wisconsin are best served by the existing state of the law, which ignores the generally accepted concept of the state university as an agency having an identity distinct from that of the state, and overlooks the fact that control of their own printing has been an attribute of most great universities, intimately connected as it is with the dissemination of the findings of their research and experimentation and the fruits of their scholarship and labors in literature and all the arts and sciences. Contrast the University of Wisconsin printing situation with the fact that many state universities own and operate not only printing establishments, but also their own radio broadcasting stations.

Relation to State's Attorney General

The Illinois decision discussed above rebuked the attorney general for asserting a right to appoint the university counsel and act as sole legal representative of the institution. The court held that the university is a public corporation constituting a legal entity distinct from that of the state, and entitled to employ its own legal counsel; and ordered the attorney general to withdraw from a pending case in a lower court where he was attempting to intrude himself as university counsel.[5]

State Institution Immune from Attachment of Funds

A creditor of two foreign corporations came into the Mississippi courts alleging that Mississippi Southern College, a state institution, owed these debtor corporations more than the amount of his claims, and invoked judicial aid to collect his claims direct from the college by statutory attachment in chancery. The college pleaded state immunity from suit, and pointed to the fact that no statute authorized it to be sued. Affirming the dismissal of the suit, the state supreme court remarked:

> An institution such as this College is entrusted only to men of high character, and they, in turn, are under the supervision of a state-wide board of trustees, selected from among the most reputable citizens of the

5 *People ex rel. Board of Trustees of University of Illinois* v. *Barrett*, 382 Ill. 321, 46 N.E. 2d 951 (1943).

state. The legislature has evidently considered that such men would be as sensitive to every financial obligation of the institution and as alert to preserve its financial integrity as would any court or jury, and that since the principal field of effort of such agency is other than business, it should not have its energies diverted by standing attendance upon litigation.

Disposal of the claim was expressly left to the discretion of the board of trustees. Neither funds appropriated to them by the state, nor funds paid into their hands by students as fees for tuition and incidentals, were subject to attachment.[6]

VALIDITY OF STATE UNIVERSITY BORROWINGS

Louisiana State University, immediately after the peculations of its president J. M. Smith came to light, refused to pay further interest on twenty-two $1,000 bonds of the university then owned by a bank which had acquired them from Smith. When sued by the bank, the university pleaded that the bonds were invalid because, although dated June 1, 1934, and having been duly authorized by a legislative act of earlier date, the bonds had not actually been sold and delivered by the university until 1936, long after a subsequent legislative act of 1935 had become law, requiring prior approval of all state agency bond issues by the State Bond and Tax Board.

The court made short shrift of this far-fetched contention, and held that the legislative act of 1935 was wholly prospective in purview, and had no effect on the validity of bonds previously authorized by the legislature. Thus a judgment for the bank was affirmed, with all the judges concurring, though Justice McCaleb registered a special concurrence in which he expressed doubt that "the holder in due course of a negotiable bond of the state or other public agency is to be accorded the same protection which is given to the holder of commercial paper issued by private individuals or corporations."[7]

The outcome of the foregoing case may have influenced Louisiana State University to elect to ground its defense on the State Bond and Tax Board Act of 1935, when another bank sued on a note for $300,000 executed by President J. M. Smith in 1939 with purported authorization by the university governing board,

6 *Smith v. Doehler Metal Furniture Co., et al.*, 195 Miss. 538, 15 So. 2d 421 (1943).
7 *State ex rel. Louisiana Savings Bank and Trust Co.* v. *Board of Supervisors of Louisiana State University*, 202 La. 176, 11 So. 2d 521 (1942).

but in fact not so authorized. Smith had obtained the sum and paid it over to his brokers, without the knowledge of the university. When sued on the note, the university chose to aver that it was invalid and unenforceable because not authorized by the State Bond and Tax Board as required by the act of 1935; and this defense was held good. The plaintiff bank contended (1) that the act of 1935 was unconstitutional as a delegation of legislative power, (2) that it did not apply to the university, and (3) if it did apply to the university it was to that extent repealed by implication by an act of 1936 which expressly gave the university broad borrowing powers. The court saw no merit in any of these contentions. The act of 1935 applied to "political and public corporations," and the university is, indeed, a public corporation, of legislative creation and control.[8]

MUNICIPAL INSTITUTIONS ARE STATE AGENCIES

In two New York cases the principle was reaffirmed that the Board of Higher Education of the City of New York is a corporate entity quite distinct from the municipal corporation, and is an agency of the state and not of the city. Thus employees of the public colleges under the jurisdiction of the Board of Higher Education are not entangled in the red tape of city ordinances applicable to city employees.[9] And the same colleges are parts of the public educational system of the state, and controversies within them are appealable to the State Commissioner of Education acting in his quasi-judicial capacity, to the same extent as disputes in other public schools of the state.[10]

In a Michigan decision it was also reaffirmed that the Board of Education of the City of Detroit, governing Wayne University, is a state agency.[11] It is worthy of careful note that the so-called "municipal" universities mentioned herein are not "municipal" in the sense of being departments of their respective city governments; they are agencies of the state—not of the city—

[8] *National Bank of Commerce in New Orleans* v. *Board of Supervisors of Louisiana State University and Agricultural and Mechanical College*, 206 La. 913, 20 So. 2d 264 (1944).

[9] *Nelson* v. *Board of Higher Education of the City of New York*, 288 N.Y. 649, 42 N.E. 2d 744 (1943).

[10] *Board of Higher Education of the City of New York* v. *Cole*, 288 N.Y. 607, 42 N.E. 2d 609 (1942).

[11] *Daszkiewicz* v. *Board of Education of City of Detroit*, 301 Mich. 212, 3 N.W. 2d 71 (1942).

and their governing boards have a corporate existence distinct from that of the city corporation.

Other litigation affecting municipal colleges and universities receives attention in Chapters IV and XVIII of this book.

PART THREE
Privately Controlled Institutions
.·.
CHAPTER VIII
SOME PRIVILEGES, POWERS, AND LIABILITIES OF PRIVATELY CONTROLLED INSTITUTIONS

CASES touching directly the incorporation and regulation of privately controlled colleges and universities were rare during this period. The privilege of tax exemption is treated in later chapters herein, as is also the subject of liability for torts. Moreover, almost every case in which such an institution is a party throws some light on its legal rights and obligations. Hence the present brief chapter is scarcely more than a reference point at which observation of the numerous cases relating to its subject may be conveniently begun.

MAY PRIVATE INSTITUTIONS ADMIT OR EXCLUDE WHOM THEY WILL?

The conservative legal view is that privately controlled educational institutions are within their rights in exercising selection —even arbitrarily—as to whom they will admit or exclude as a student, because no one can claim admission as of right. It is no secret that some heavily endowed universities and colleges have often contrived by more or less covert but none the less efficacious means to discourage and prevent the entrance of more than limited quotas of students of Jewish extraction, or others whose race or religion differentiated them from the majority of the institution's clientele. Straws in the wind of 1945 indicate a brewing change. We have already noticed that a New York statute forbids nonsectarian tax-exempt institutions to reject qualified applicants solely on account of their race, color, or religion; and that a suit brought thereunder in 1945 failed to reach the merits of the matter because the petitioner was not an aggrieved party and did not allege any specific positive violation of the statute.[1]

---

[1] *Goldstein* v. *Mills et al.*, 185 Misc. 851, 57 N.Y.S. 2d 810 (1945); affirmed without opinion, 62 N.Y.S. 2d 619 (1946).

Another straw is the Enoch Pratt Free Library case, also discussed in Chapter II of this volume, wherein a federal court definitively held that the policy of excluding qualified applicants from the library training class solely because they are Negroes is a violation of the United States Constitution and cannot stand.[2] The library trustees constitute a private nonprofit educational corporation with full power to manage the institution, although title to its physical plant is held by the city of Baltimore, and by long custom of the city provides from public funds a major portion of the annual operating budget. Neither of these two circumstances, in the older legal view, would have altered or affected the privileges and powers of the private corporation; but now they are used, logically enough, to support the judicial conclusion that the library is thereby so much an agency of the state that it is subject to the same constitutional restraints as the state itself. From this decision it is not an overlong step to a similar conclusion regarding any private nonprofit educational institution, for all are in a sense agencies of the state performing a public service, and all receive aid from the state in the shape of tax exemptions which are the practical equivalent of pecuniary subsidies.

Transfer of Assets
to Similar Corporation in Another State

More than twenty years ago a majority of the trustees of the Meadville Theological School in Pennsylvania determined to transfer the institution to the vicinity of the University of Chicago on account of the advantages of proximity to a great university in a metropolitan center. In the ensuing litigation the supreme court of Pennsylvania decided that there was no barrier to prevent the desired transfer of all the educational activities of the institution, but that under its charter the trustees would be required to hold at least one meeting annually in Meadville, and maintain the corporation office nominally there; and they could not lawfully transfer the corporate assets to a new corporation in Illinois unless and until the old corporation should be lawfully dissolved.

After conducting the activities of the institution in Chicago

---

[2] *Kerr et al.* v. *Enoch Pratt Free Library of Baltimore City et al.*, (U.S.C.C.A.), 149 F. 2d 212 (1945). Certiorari denied, 326 U.S. 721, 66 S. Ct. 26, 90 L. Ed. 36 (1945).

for nearly two decades, the trustees again petitioned in 1943 for permission to transfer the institution's endowment and other assets to Lombard College, an existing Illinois corporation, alleging that the two schools have the same trustees and officers, the same faculty, and occupy the same buildings; their corporate purposes are substantially the same, and their bylaws practically identical; and union would result in tax savings and be otherwise advantageous to their charter purposes. Dismissal of the petition by the Pennsylvania Court of Common Pleas was affirmed by the state supreme court, on the ground that it was an attempt to relitigate a question previously adjudicated finally, and therefore barred by the rule of *res judicata.*[3]

INVESTMENT OF ENDOWMENT IN DORMITORIES

Judicial pronouncements directing college trustees with reference to the investment of endowment funds under their control are so rare that they are seized upon with avidity by persons bearing such responsibilities. One such pronouncement comes from a Baltimore court which was called upon to determine the legality of the plan of the trustees of Goucher College to invest a portion of that institution's endowment funds in the erection and furnishing of new dormitories. The plan contemplated that the income from the operation of the projected dormitories would produce a reasonable return on the investment and would also enable it to be amortized at the rate of not less than 2 percent each year, so that the entire principal would be repaid within the estimated useful life of the buildings. The amount immediately involved was about $216,000 out of a present endowment aggregating nearly $2,500,000.

The court noted that the plan was an essential part of the current transfer of the Goucher campus from a location in the city, which had become congested and unsuitable, to a larger and more appropriate location outside the city. It observed also that successful investments in income-producing residence halls on their own campuses have been made by such institutions as Dartmouth, Bryn Mawr, Stanford, Northwestern, and Vanderbilt. Concluding that this type of investment is eminently proper

---

3 *Hempstead* v. *Meadville Theological School,* 346 Pa. 276, 29 A. 2d 509 (1943), with reference to *Same,* 284 Pa. 147, 130 A. 421 (1925), and 286 Pa. 493, 134 A. 103, 49 A.L.R. 1145 (1926).

and prudent under the circumstances, the court added a clear statement of the general rule governing investments by trustees:[4]

> Unless it is otherwise provided by the terms of the trust or by statute, the trustees are under a duty to make such investments as a prudent man would make of his own property, having primarily in view the preservation of the trust estate and the amount and regularity of the income to be derived.

Investment of endowment in income-producing dormitories is not to be confused, of course, with borrowing from endowment to finance classroom buildings or other plant facilities from which no cash income is probable, or with borrowing from endowment to pay current operating expenses. Both of these latter practices are generally imprudent, and each has hastened the demise of many a financially anemic institution.

[4] *Ex parte Goucher College*, Circuit Court No. 2 of Baltimore City. Decree of June 7, 1941.

PART FOUR

Fiscal Relationships with Governmental Units

∴

CHAPTER IX

CHARTER EXEMPTIONS FROM TAXATION

WHERE the charter of an institution embodies an explicit grant of exemption from taxation, the case is distinct from the instances wherein only the application of an exemption provided by a general statute is at issue.

Authorities are agreed that the charter is a contract between the state and the institution; this may restrain the state but little if by the terms of the charter the state reserves to itself the right to amend or repeal it. Charters granted subsequently to the adoption of state constitutional limitations of the legislative power cannot overstep those limitations; but charters antedating such limitations, if granted without reservation, are unaffected by them; for in such a case the charter is a contract whose obligation the United States Constitution forbids any state to impair.

There is respectable minority opinion, however, that the alienation of its taxing power is a matter in which a state cannot bind itself by contract. Examples of all these theories appear in recent decisions.

CHARTER EXEMPTIONS RESTRICTED

Elon College, having been ordered by a court to pay local taxes assessed for the years 1938–40 against an office building owned by it and rented to commercial tenants in Reidsville, North Carolina, appealed to the state supreme court, pointing to its charter of 1889 which provided that its "property to the amount of $500,000 shall forever be exempt from taxation," and an amendment of 1917 which raised the limit to $5,000,000. Its total current holdings did not exceed $1,500,000 in value. Moreover, the state constitution provides that "property held for educational, literary, charitable, or scientific purposes" may be exempted from taxation by the General Assembly, and a statute recites that "property beneficially belonging to or held for the benefit of . . . educational . . . institutions . . . where the rent, interest or income from such investments shall be used exclusively for . . . educational . . . purposes" shall be exempt.

Making the narrowest possible interpretation of the constitutional provision, the court construed it to include only the campus and educational buildings and not the office building held as an investment. The college, said the court, "is entitled to exemption on the campus and is liable to tax in the market place." As to the charter, the decision held that the exemption clause is restricted by the constitutional requirement that "taxes on property shall be uniform as to each class of property taxed," and emphasized that the office building was in a business district where it competed with other property similarly situated and shared equally in community benefits, and hence should bear its part of the public burdens.[1] This is a strictly literal and unimaginative application of the theory that "exemptions are not allowed as releases *in personam*, but are confined to releases *in rem*, based on the purpose for which the *res* is held." It views the purpose of the building as income-producing or gainful, and ignores the fact that the gains are dedicated to a nonprofit purpose.

In a contemporaneous case in which Guilford College sought to recover taxes paid under protest, the North Carolina court followed the same doctrine and held taxable two houses and lots situated at a distance from the campus and rented to persons not connected with the college. Concerning the Dolly Madison birthplace at this institution, a small brick house and lot only 300 yards from the campus entrance and occupied by a member of the faculty whose salary is adjusted to allow for the rental, the court felt uncertain and accordingly remanded this part of the case for further proceedings to amplify the facts.[2] In each of the North Carolina cases Justice Seawell dissented without opinion.

EXEMPTIONS FULLY SUSTAINED

William Jewell College brought an action in equity to declare void the assessment of real estate taxes on its lands in Worth County which had been acquired from a debtor of the college in

---

[1] *Rockingham County* v. *Board of Trustees of Elon College*, 219 N.C. 342, 13 S.E. 2d 618 (1941).

[2] *Trustees of Guilford College* v. *Guilford County et al.*, 219 N.C. 347, 13 S.E. 2d 622 (1941).

settlement of a mortgage. The college alleged that its practice was not to invest endowment funds in real estate, except to protect its loans, and that it did not customarily hold such real estate longer than necessary to procure a proper sale. A broad exemption clause in the college charter of 1849, as amended in 1851, was relied on, and sustained by the supreme court of Missouri as a contract inviolable under that clause of the United States Constitution which prohibits the states from impairing the obligation of a contract.[3] Chief Justice Ellison dissented without opinion. The opposing argument, made with no avail, was that the Missouri general corporation act of 1845 reserved to the state the right to alter or repeal charters granted under it; and the William Jewell College charter was actually amended by successive new state constitutions of 1865 and 1875, both of which restricted the field within which the legislature could grant tax exemptions. This is the same argument that has repeatedly come to naught in earlier similar cases in Missouri courts and in federal courts.

Hamline University, in Minnesota, has a Territorial charter of 1854, stipulating that "all corporate property belonging to the institution, both real and personal, is and shall be free from taxation." Relying on this clause, the university sued to register clear title to tax-delinquent lands in Hennepin and Ramsey counties, held as investments and not physically used for educational purposes. The Minnesota supreme court decided that the charter exemption was a contract which the state could not impair. The conclusion is in harmony with earlier precedents in Minnesota as well as in Missouri. The contract was unaffected by the adoption of the state constitution of 1857, and was not avoided by the fact that Hamline University suspended operation from 1869 to 1880, because the charter was never repealed nor revoked, and the period of suspension was not sufficient to work a forfeiture of the charter by non-user.

Taking cognizance of the Phillips Exeter case of 1940, the Minnesota court ingeniously distinguished it from the present case by pointing out that there the charter exemption was an act of 1781, "before New Hampshire became a state and before our national constitution was adopted." And "There the grant

---

[3] *Trustees of William Jewell College of Liberty* v. *Beavers,* 351 Mo. 87, 171 S.W. 2d 604 (1943).

was declared void because the assembly granting it was only a delegated agency and for that reason could not enact irrevocable laws. . . . Our case is founded on an entirely different base. Here there was a grant by the representatives of the people under the powers conferred by the federal government."[4]

The point of distinction is not as satisfying as might be desired. No legislature can enact "irrevocable laws"; it can only bind the state by enacting the state's commitment to a contract with another party; and it could be very strongly argued that New Hampshire was a state in the generic sense in 1781, capable of binding itself by contract through the agency of its delegate assembly. But this has little to do with the basic theory of the Exeter case, which was that the taxing power is so essential an element of the state's power that it cannot be alienated in perpetuity. It remains to be seen how this theory will fare in the courts in future years.

CHARTER EXEMPTION MUST BE EXPLICIT AND NOT VAGUELY IMPORTED

Evidently emboldened by the success of William Jewell College in having its charter exemption reaffirmed in full, Central College, another Missouri institution, sought to have assessments for 1943 of its lands held as endowment declared illegal and void. The lands had been acquired between 1929 and 1932, and the annual taxes on all lands owned by the college were now approximately $8,000. The only arguments available to the college involved a species of far-fetched osmosis, as follows: Its charter of 1855 contained no mention of tax exemption, but gave it "all the rights, powers and privileges usually enjoyed by colleges and universities of the highest grade, or which may be necessary and proper to enable them to promote the cause of learning in the state." In substance the contention was that the Missouri act of 1851 which amended the William Jewell College charter of 1849 by providing for total exemption from taxation, was a general act in force when the 1855 charter of Central College was enacted; and since both related to higher education in

---

[4] *Trustees of Hamline University* v. *Peacock*, 217 Minn. 399, 14 N.W. 2d 773 (1944); certiorari denied, *State of Minnesota* v. *Hamline University of Minnesota*, 323 U.S. 741, 65 S. Ct. 73, 89 L. Ed. 593 (1944).

the state, they should be read *in pari materia*, and the act of 1851 should be read into the act of 1855.

This argument contained the seeds of its own defeat. Carefully abstaining from deciding whether the act of 1851 was a general act or not, and thus giving Central College the greatest possible benefit of doubt, the court pointed out that if it were a general act, then it was assuredly repealed by the constitutional changes of 1865 and 1875 which restricted the power of the legislature to grant exemptions. "No person has a vested right in any general rule of law or policy of legislation entitling him to insist that it shall remain unchanged for his benefit." Moreover, "an immunity from a change of the general rules of law will not ordinarily be implied as an unexpressed term of an express contract." Thus the exemption of William Jewell College by act of 1851 could not be imported into the Central College charter act of 1855; and if the act of 1851 was ever intended to be a general act, it has long since been repealed as such; though it remains perpetually in force as a special act relating to William Jewell College, "because it is an express term of the contract between that college and the state."[5] The United States Supreme Court has decided that there was no substantial federal question involved in the Central College case.

[5] *Curators of Central College* v. *Rose*, 182 S.W. 2d 145 (1945); appeal dismissed for want of a substantial federal question, 323 U.S. 678, 65 S. Ct. 269, 89 L. Ed. 550 (1944); and rehearing denied, 323 U.S. 818, 65 S. Ct. 429, 89 L. Ed. 650 (1945).

CHAPTER X
EXEMPTION FROM PROPERTY TAXES UNDER
GENERAL STATUTES

GENERAL statutes providing for tax exemption of educational institutions perennially require judicial interpretation of their application to different types of institutional property used for varying purposes and held under diverse circumstances and conditions.

CAMPUS AND PHYSICAL PLANT

A war-born case in Florida required a decision as to whether the plant of the Riverside Military Academy, regularly exempt from taxation, became taxable in 1943 when seized by the United States Government for use by the Navy. The Florida supreme court readily decided that the school plant was not taxable while the regular activities of the school were suspended and the property was pre-empted for Navy use in furthering the war effort.[1]

Oral negotiations with Navy officers regarding lease of the plant did not eventuate in the execution and delivery of a written contract, and consequently the Government's entry was by a condemnation proceeding under the Second War Powers Act, with rental to be determined by a jury.[2]

In New Hampshire the historic exemption of "seminaries of learning" extends to an additional $150,000 worth of real estate not a part of the seminary, if "owned and occupied by them, their officers, or their students for the purposes for which they are established." Mount Saint Mary College is an institution of the Sisters of Mercy in the town of Hookset, who also own other educational and charitable properties in the towns of Hookset, Nashua, and Manchester. The New Hampshire supreme court decided that the college is undoubtedly a "seminary of learning," as is also the normal school for novitiates in Manchester; and, by a common-sense construction of the $150,000 exemption, declared that "to the extent that the plaintiffs have had the bene-

[1] *Watkins* v. *Riverside Military Academy*, 155 Fla. 283, 23 So. 2d 386 (1945).
[2] *U. S. A.* v. *Certain Lands in Hollywood, Broward County, Florida, Riverside Military Academy, et al.*, (U.S.D.C.), 53 F. Supp. 124 (1943).

fit of this institutional exemption elsewhere [in other towns], they may not have it in Hookset." In other words, $150,000 is the limit of value, whether located in one town or in several.

The judges disagreed on what should be the measure of value. Should it be (1) what the college could obtain for the property if sold on assessment day, or (2) replacement cost, less depreciation? The majority decided in favor of sale value, coupled with a statement that replacement cost might properly be taken into consideration "in cases where sale value is not an adequate measure." One judge dissented, insisting that the test should be what the college would be willing to pay rather than lose the property in question. All agreed that land unused for any purpose is taxable, as also is property rented out for income; and part of the campus used as a golf course is exempt as a part of the seminary.[3]

HOUSES FOR PRESIDENT AND PROFESSORS

In 1939 the trustees of Rutgers University acquired an eleven-acre tract on which was situated a large dwelling house, the purpose being to provide a residence for the president of the university near the campus. The property was assessed for taxation in 1940 by Piscataway Township, and the university thereupon asked the Board of Tax Appeals to set aside the assessment on the building and five acres of the curtilage, on the ground that the property is exempt from taxation under the well-known New Jersey statute exempting college buildings and land necessary to the fair enjoyment thereof, not exceeding five acres in extent.

Upon evidence that the house is actually used almost daily not merely as a private home for the president and his family, but for housing guests of the university, dinner meetings of various administrative, faculty, and student organizations and groups, and meetings of the board of trustees, and the trustees had enlarged its kitchen and dining-room facilities to suit those very purposes, it was readily concluded that the assessment should be set aside, as to the building and five acres.[4]

---

[3] *Sisters of Mercy v. Town of Hookset*, 93 N.H. 301, 42 A. 2d 222 (1945).

[4] *Trustees of Rutgers College v. Piscataway Township*, 20 N.J. Misc. 127, 25 A. 2d 248 (1942); affirmed, 129 N.J.L. 261, 29 A. 2d 389 (1942), and 131 N.J.L. 158, 35 A. 2d 711 (1944).

In 1942 the supreme court of Georgia held that several dwelling houses owned by Atlanta University and situated immediately across the street from its main campus, and occupied as residences by members of the faculty rent-free, were exempt from taxation. The value of the perquisite was taken into account in determining faculty salaries, and it was shown that the houses were frequently used for conferences between students and faculty members.

In the same case it was also determined that a vacant lot, in close proximity to other buildings used for college purposes, being too small for a regular football field or baseball diamond, and actually used only by students for playing outdoor games, is properly exempt.[5]

Cases involving dormitories, union buildings, and fraternity houses are discussed in Chapter XXI, Accessory Educational Corporations and Associations.

REAL PROPERTY HELD AS INVESTMENT

In some states lands or buildings held by a college solely as a form of investment, and not themselves used for any educational purpose, are taxable. Oklahoma now joins that category by virtue of a 1945 decision overruling earlier cases to the contrary, and putting a new interpretation on the exemption statute.

A farm owned by Phillips University and rented out, the income being devoted exclusively to the general purposes of the university, was assessed for 1945. The university could point to the 1930 case of *Garfield County* v. *Phillips University* as a precedent for its exemption; but this argument was effective only up to the time of the decision of the 1945 case of *Oklahoma County* v. *Queen City Lodge, I.O.O.F.*, by which the Garfield County case was overruled and the principle asserted that hereafter the statutory exemption of educational and charitable institutions will apply only to property owned and physically used by them for their stated purposes. The Queen City Lodge case decided that where the lodge owned a twelve-story building and occupied only the twelfth floor, renting out the remaining floors and de-

---

[5] *Elder et al.* v. *Trustees of Atlanta University*, 194 Ga. 716, 22 S.E. 2d 515, 143 A.L.R. 268 (1942).

voting the proceeds to its charitable purposes, only the twelfth floor was exempt from taxation. It was small comfort to Phillips University that the overturning of the established precedent was held to have no retroactive effect, thus permitting the university to win its point regarding the assessment for 1945. The court made it clear that the result would have been opposite if taxation for 1946 or a subsequent year had been at issue.[6]

Kentucky provides an example of steadfast continuance of a more liberal view of investment property. When the city of Louisville attempted in 1943 to assess for taxation all income-producing real estate within its limits owned by charitable and educational institutions, the Court of Appeals decided that the judicial interpretation of Section 170 of the Kentucky constitution under which such property has been held exempt in a chain of decisions since 1896 should be maintained:

> Property rights have vested on the faith of that construction. Devises of real estate to charitable and educational institutions have been made, and such institutions have invested portions of their endowment funds in real estate in the belief that such property was exempt from taxation. To make it subject to taxation would materially impair its value and in many instances would adversely affect the activities of the institution.

Luridly phrased arguments of counsel for the city were considerably deflated by the court's calmly pointing to the fact that in 1944 all the real property in Louisville owned by charitable and educational institutions aggregated less than three-fourths of one per cent of the total value of taxable property.[7]

PROPERTY AFFECTED WITH A PRIVATE INTEREST

The courts naturally scrutinize closely any exemption of college property in which a private individual has retained an interest. Thus at Miami University, where a fourteen-acre part of the campus had been conveyed to the university by two grantors under a deed reserving to them the right to live in a house on the premises for the duration of their lives, free of rent and with heating furnished by the university, and forbidding

---

[6] *Gibson* v. *Phillips University*, 195 Okla. 456, 158 P. 2d 901 (1945).

[7] *City of Louisville* v. *Presbyterian Orphans' Home Society of Louisville et al.*, 299 Ky. 566, 186 S.W. 2d 194 (1945).

use of this house by the university during that time, the Ohio supreme court sustained a tax board ruling that the house and the one acre on which it stood were taxable in the names of the owners of the life estate. The remainder of the fourteen-acre tract, being used for housing and training Navy radio students, was properly exempt. "The residence not being used for any purpose connected with the university and not being open to the public generally, is in fact used for a private purpose."[8]

A more difficult case arose under the Iowa statute exempting "real estate owned by any educational institution of this state as part of its endowment fund, to the extent of 160 acres in any civil township." A quarter block in downtown Des Moines, occupied by two department stores, was conveyed to Grinnell College at a price of $330,000, to be paid at the rate of $1,000 a month for life to each of the three grantors, or at such rate as the income would make possible after April 1, 1955; plus other payments to named beneficiaries aggregating $4,500 a year if the net income were sufficient. The question was whether this transaction was a sale actually transferring the beneficial interest in the property as well as the legal title to the college, or whether instead it merely created a trust for the benefit of the private parties. An actuary testified that the net assessed value of the property was slightly less than the sum that would be required to purchase the annuities from an insurance company.

The court intimated that it suspected a device to avoid income taxes, and concluded that the transaction created an express trust for the benefit of private parties; that the college does not own the property in a sense sufficient to justify its exemption under the statute. The majority pointed out that all the payments except the three annuities until 1955 are, strictly speaking, earnings and not annuities; but "where a trustee is required to make payments to beneficiaries it is not very material by what name such payments are designated." Three of the judges dissented, arguing that the transaction should be regarded as a purchase, pure and simple, creating a debt and not a trust. Less impressed than their colleagues by the hint of income tax evasion, the minority judges pointed out that the payments to the grantors are

[8] *President and Trustees of Miami University* v. *Evatt*, 144 Ohio St. 434, 59 N.E. 2d 366 (1945).

taxable in their names under an Iowa statute taxing "moneys and credits."[9]

PROPERTY IN HANDS OF LONG-TERM LESSEES

Certain public lands granted to the state of Ohio for Miami University more than a century ago are expressly exempted by statute from "state taxes." Long ago the lands were let to long-term lessees, and local taxes have always been paid by the lessees. In 1935 an appellate court confirmed this practice by holding that "state taxes" as used in the statute meant only levies by the state and not levies by local subdivisions. Subsequently some of the lessees sought to escape the taxes by asserting that they should be assessed against the university as lessor. The Ohio supreme court held that the lessees are liable for the taxes.[10]

PROPERTY IN HANDS OF SPECIAL TRUSTEE

The city and school district of Fort Worth sued to collect personal property taxes for 1941 on notes and mortgages payable to the Mary Couts Burnett Trust, set up in 1923 to hold and operate a large estate until 20 years after the death of the last survivor who signed the trust indenture. The corpus was then to go to Texas Christian University. Meantime, three-fourths of the income was to be paid annually to Mrs. Burnett during her life, and thereafter all income to the university. Mrs. Burnett died prior to this suit.

The Texas constitution and statutes exempt from taxation "the endowment funds of institutions of learning and religion not used with a view to profit." Real property acquired by foreclosure is exempt for two years only. The Texas supreme court decided that since the income from the notes and mortgages in question went into a common fund which was paid annually to Texas Christian University after expenses were deducted, the instruments were properly exempt from taxation. The income cannot inure to the private profit of any individual, and "private profit," not merely "profit," is what is meant to be excepted by

[9] *Trustees of Iowa College (official name of Grinnell College)* v. *Baillie*, (Ia.), 17 N.W. 2d 143 (1945).
[10] *Cordes* v. *DuBois*, 136 Ohio St. 573, 27 N.E. 2d 405 (1941), affirming *Same*, (Ohio App.), 34 N.E. 2d 245 (1939).

the constitution and statutes; for the sole purpose of an endowment fund is to produce income.[11]

Property Owned by a Charitable Corporation and Destined for Charitable Use at an Undetermined Future Time

The Ohio supreme court has long been accustomed to holding, under the pertinent sections of the state constitution and statutes, that real or personal property owned by a charitable institution is not exempt from taxation unless and until it is being exclusively used for charitable purposes. In harmony with the precedents in that state is a 1943 decision that the funds of a charitable corporation which conducts no charitable activities directly, but merely makes gifts to other charitable enterprises, meantime investing its funds and accumulating dividends and interest therefrom, are taxable. "The charitable use of appellant's assets begins only after appellant parts with the title and possession of such property to another charitable institution."[12]

Likewise Ohio holds that land acquired by a nonprofit educational corporation with intent to build and operate a school thereon is not exempt from taxation during the intervening period, and is taxable until its actual and immediate use as the site of an educational "going concern" begins.[13]

Tests of Nonprofit Charitable Character

The World Wide Broadcasting Foundation of Massachusetts is a stock corporation created in 1942. Its only shareholder was the World Wide Broadcasting Foundation, Inc., a New York corporation established in 1935 to create a "world wide university of the air," with the aid of an initial grant from the Rockefeller Foundation. In 1936 this parent corporation moved its headquarters to Boston and constructed short-wave radio station WROL in Scituate. One of the courses broadcast was Basic English, intended primarily for South Americans.

[11] *Harris et al.* v. *City of Fort Worth et al.*, 142 Tex. 589, 180 S.W. 2d 131 (1944); reversing *Same*, (Tex. Civ. App.), 177 S.W. 2d 308 (1944).

[12] *Wehrle Foundation* v. *Evatt et al.*, 141 Ohio St. 467, 49 N.E. 2d 52 (1943).

[13] *Ursuline Academy of Cleveland* v. *Board of Tax Appeals et al.*, 141 Ohio St. 563, 49 N.E. 2d 674 (1943).

Real property on Commonwealth Avenue in Boston, owned and occupied by the Massachusetts corporation as the center of the "World Wide University of the Air," was assessed for 1943 as taxable; and the corporation sued for abatement of the tax. The charters of both corporations stated identical purposes: To develop, produce, and broadcast radio or television programs of cultural, educational, artistic, or spiritual nature throughout the world; to issue books and pamphlets relating thereto; and to acquire, use, and transfer radio facilities or other property of any kind. Neither charter nor by-laws made any provision regarding distribution of profits or income. The assessors contended that it could not be shown that there was anything to prevent dissolution and division of assets, if any.

The court looked beyond this contention to the substance, and found that there were no profits; that no commerical sponsorship or advertising was accepted; that under war restriction of foreign broadcasting, the Foundation assisted the Government in preparing foreign broadcast materials; and that it subsisted on gifts and grants, the Carnegie Endowment for International Peace having been one of the contributors. The court concluded "No other objects or purposes than those set forth in the charter could be engaged in validly, and those objects and purposes are exclusively charitable in character"; and, from reading the charter, "We are persuaded that in all its implications a profit-making institution was not contemplated." On this basis the decision in favor of exemption was made. "We are not called upon," said the court, "to decide how disposition of property should be made, should its purposes cease to be susceptible of execution according to their foundation."[14]

Courts are inclined to look to the realities characterizing an institution's operation, and reluctant to recognize a right to exemption when there is evidence that one of its principal purposes is to provide a livelihood for its "leading spirits." Thus exemption of the 18-room dwelling which housed the College of Paterson, a two-year institution in New Jersey, was denied, although the school was organized as a nonprofit corporation, had never operated at a profit, and paid only very modest salaries. The court noted that the building was used as permanent living

[14] *Assessors of Boston* v. *World Wide Broadcasting Foundation of Massachusetts,* 317 Mass. 598, 59 N.E. 2d 188 (1945).

quarters by the president and his wife (who served as registrar), and by the bursar and his wife; and the evidence did not disclose that any scholarships had ever been provided. In these circumstances the college was held to have "failed to sustain the burden of proving its right to exemption."[15]

A seemingly strict interpretation of what is educational and charitable appeared in an Ohio supreme court decision refusing exemption of a building in Cleveland housing a small Orthodox Jewish theological seminary operated by an Ohio nonprofit corporation known as the American Committee of the Rabbinical College of Telshe, Inc., and containing sleeping, dining, study, and lecture facilities for students and teachers, and a synagogue attended by some residents of the vicinity. Students paid no fees for tuition or rooms, and only ten percent of them paid anything for meals, the principal source of support being donations from alumni and others. The teachers were two rabbis, who jointly held legal title to the property in trust for the corporation. The method of selecting students for admission did not appear in the record. Possibly that factor was influential in the unanimous decision that "the use disclosed by the record is private in character," and that the property was not devoted to a charitable use, "nor even to an exclusively religious use."[16]

[15] *College of Paterson* v. *State Board of Tax Appeals et al.*, 131 N.J.L. 57, 34 A. 2d 740 (1943).
[16] *Bloch* v. *Board of Tax Appeals*, 144 Ohio St. 414, 59 N.E. 2d 145 (1945).

CHAPTER XI
PROPERTY TAX EXEMPTION OF VARIOUS TYPES OF INSTITUTIONS

IN surprisingly many instances it is difficult to distinguish whether a particular institution at a particular time is proprietary or nonprofit. Likewise the precise line of demarcation between what is educational and what is not is often hard to trace. In this chapter we look at proprietary institutions in transition to nonprofit status; business colleges; libraries; agricultural fair associations; professional societies; and a variety of recreational and cultural enterprises whose activities partake to some extent of the characteristics of an educational institution.

If any of these instances seems far afield from the realm of higher education as conventionally conceived, let it be remembered that no university or college can afford to ignore the numerous worthy agencies of informal education, or to suppose that the field is neatly and completely preempted by formal institutionalized education in the traditional mold and manner.

REORGANIZED BUSINESS COLLEGES

It frequently happens that proprietary schools seek to change their status to that of nonprofit institutions. Since this involves important modifications of their organization and operation, and often requires considerable time, the question of whether and when it has been accomplished sometime presents difficulties.

Rider College at Trenton, New Jersey, has been operated since 1865. It was incorporated in 1897. By-laws adopted at an uncertain date provide for a so-called "endowment fund" to consist of all receipts in excess of the operating expenses and restrict the use of the principal to necessary enlargement of the college facilities and payment of debts, and "such other purposes as the board of governors may unanimously determine." It was in fact a proprietary business college until 1935, when it purchased the equities of the two deceased owner-partners for $98,000 cash and a substantial mortgage. In 1937 a clause prohibiting private gain from its operation was inserted in its charter. By 1940 the mortgage had been reduced to approximately $39,000, and the "endowment fund" amounted to about $165,000. The state board of tax appeals determined that it was exempt from taxation and cancelled assessments against its property for the year 1940, but on appeal to the supreme court the decision was reversed.

The opinion by Judge Perskie emphasized that the by-laws and charter provisions relied upon for exemption were revocable and that the "endowment fund" was in fact not an endowment but merely a reserve fund. He thought there was not sufficient evidence of change in the institution's *modus operandi* to make it clearly nonprofit and charitable. He was influenced by the fact that the college was paying annual salaries of $8,400 to its president and dean, both of whom were sons of the original proprietors; by the fact that there was an operating surplus or profit of $17,000 for the year 1939–1940; and by evidence that Negro applicants were discouraged if not actually barred from admission.[1]

In view of the fact that the decision was subsequently affirmed without opinion by the Court of Errors and Appeals, Judge Perskie's words on the latter point are of special interest as further evidence of a rising judicial tendency to look askance at racial discrimination, already noticed herein in earlier chapters:

> The proof is plenary that it is respondent's policy not to accept Negro students. Out of an enrollment of 1,200 students . . . there was not one Negro student enrolled with respondent on October 1, 1939, and for ten years prior thereto respondent had but 'four or five' Negro students, all of whom attended evening sessions. The explanation given is that respondent has 'no facilities for the placement of Negro students after graduation.' There is nothing to indicate that respondent is either obliged to, or does, place all of its graduates. That explanation, to say the least, can hardly be said to indicate a fundamentally charitable or philanthropic basis of operation.

Whether a "business college" is within the meaning of tax exemption statutes applicable to "schools and colleges" has been frequently disputed. The supreme court of Washington holds that such an institution in Seattle, recently reorganized as a nonprofit corporation and owning a four-story building, all of which is used for educational purposes except a portion of the ground floor leased to commercial firms, is entitled under Washington statutes to exemption from taxation of all its personal property,

---

[1] *City of Trenton v. State Board of Tax Appeals and Rider College*, 127 N.J.L. 105, 21 A. 2d 644 (1941), affirmed without opinion, 128 N.J.L. 320, 25 A. 2d 630 (1942).

of the part of its building used for educational purposes, and of a proportionate fraction of the land on which the building stands.[2] Chief Justice Blake, dissenting, maintained the view that the rule of strict construction of tax-exemption statutes should be adhered to.

Proprietary Business Colleges

The taxability of real property of which the Massey Business College (a partnership) was lessee was at issue in an Alabama decision of 1945. The owner of the three-story building in Birmingham rented the first floor for commercial uses, and the upper two floors to the business college. The whole building was assessed at $54,000, but the local circuit court ordered the upper floors exempted and fixed the assessed value of the remainder at $40,500. This judgment was reversed by the Alabama supreme court, which held that there is no division of a building by floors for tax purposes in that state, without mentioning the fact that such division is common practice in many other states. The question of whether a proprietary business college is a "school" within the meaning of the exemption clauses of the constitution and statutes was regarded by the court as debatable, and decision of the point was expressly avoided.[3]

A clear-cut decision of virtually the same question was made by the Oregon supreme court in a 1944 case wherein the property of the Behnke-Walker Business College was declared taxable because it was operated for private gain, and the exemption of "literary, benevolent, charitable, and scientific institutions" was held not to cover proprietary enterprises. In this conclusion Judge Kelly concurred specially, in a lengthy opinion developing the thesis that a business college is not a literary or scientific institution.[4]

When Is a Library Public?

The Pierpont Morgan Library in New York City was established in 1924 as a public library under a special legislative charter. It was tax exempt until 1935, when the tax authorities asserted that it was in fact not a public library, because of its very

2 *Wilson's Modern Business College* v. *King County,* 4 Wash. 2d 636, 104 P. 2d 580 (1940).
3 *State* v. *Bridges,* (Ala.), 21 So. 2d 316 (1945).
4 *Behnke-Walker Business College* v. *Multnomah County,* 173 Ore. 510, 146 P. 2d 614 (1944).

limited use. It consists of a rare and valuable collection, open only to accredited persons who apply in writing. The general trial court curtly disposed of the matter by declaring that the rules under which the library operates are reasonable and not discriminatory, and pointed out that no instance in which any member of the public had been denied admission was in evidence. Accordingly the institution was held to be properly exempt from taxation.[5]

"Literary and Scientific Institutions"

A Maine statute exempts from taxation "the real estate of all literary and scientific institutions occupied by them for their own purposes or by any officer thereof as a residence . . .; but so much of the real estate of such corporations as is not occupied by them for their own purposes shall be taxed in the municipality in which it is situated." An interesting case involved the status under this statute of a fairground at the city of Lewiston. The court readily reached the conclusion that the annual agricultural fair is a scientific institution, and that the fairground in general, including race track, grandstand, stables, and several other buildings and appurtenances, is tax exempt. Further, the fact that the association owning the property sometimes uses or permits it to be used when the annual fair is not in progress, for pari-mutuel horse races, rodeos, circuses, shows, and amusements, was held to be immaterial.

The exemption, however, is not without exception. One exhibition hall, which the fair association regularly operates as a year-round skating rink for revenue, is held to be taxable. Taxable also are certain parts of the fairground rented to private persons who maintain cottages upon them. The same is true of a small part which is rented to the proprietor of a "victualing house." One stable which is let to a riding master for his exclusive use as a private riding school is taxable, and also a certain part of the fairground which is vacant and not used for any purpose.[6]

A New Jersey court took a somewhat different view of an agricultural fairground owned by a Grange. Here it was held

---

[5] *People ex rel. Pierpont Morgan Library* v. *Miller et al.*, 177 Misc. 144, 29 N.Y.S. 2d 445 (1941).

[6] *City of Lewiston* v. *All Maine Fair Association*, 138 Me. 39, 21 A. 2d 625 (1941).

that the operations of numerous commercial concessionaires at the annual fair resulted in "a regular use of the property for pecuniary profit, not incidental to any proper fraternal activity, and exemption from taxation is not established." In this case the argument for exemption was grounded on the long-standing New Jersey statute exempting property of fraternal organizations when used for nonprofit purposes.[7]

PROFESSIONAL SOCIETIES

An admittedly close and difficult decision was made by the Michigan supreme court, affirming a judgment making the Engineering Society of Detroit liable for 1942 taxes on the half of the Horace H. Rackham Educational Memorial Building occupied by it. Record title to this half of the building was in the Rackham Engineering Foundation, but by virtue of its occupancy the Engineering Society was in the position of equitable owner. The other half of the building, occupied by the University of Michigan as an extension center, was not taxed.

The Engineering Society had 24 affiliate societies, and an aggregate of some 3,700 individual members, of whom about 2,000 did not belong to any affiliate. The Society and each of its affiliates had monthly meetings in the building, often with dinners. A staff of 50 employees was maintained in food service, caretaking of amusement facilities, and building maintenance. There was a small library and a librarian. It was said that the Society "sponsors courses in technical subjects such as chemistry and conducts a vocational guidance engineering program for senior high-school students." But the supreme court concluded that the activities in the building were very largely those of a social and recreational club, and did not feel that the facts would justify disturbing the lower court judgment that the property was not primarily used for educational or scientific purposes.[8]

WHAT IS AN EDUCATIONAL INSTITUTION?

Decisions by California and Kentucky courts bear on the recurrent question of what is an educational institution and what

[7] *Morris Grange, No. 105, Patrons of Husbandry,* v. *Township of Parsippany—Troy Hills,* 20 N.J. Misc. 99, 24 A. 2d 807 (1942).

[8] *Engineering Society of Detroit* v. *City of Detroit,* 308 Mich. 539, 14 N.W. 2d 79 (1944).

is not. Although the California code definition of an institution of collegiate grade contemplates either a four-year liberal arts course or a three-year course in some profession such as law, theology, or journalism, the appellate court at Los Angeles did not feel rigidly bound to the strictest literal interpretation. Thus the Pasadena Playhouse Association recovered as wrongfully collected the taxes on its seven-story building, which was used primarily for "class work and instruction," but contained an auditorium in which regular paid performances were given; more than half of the actors appearing therein were non-students. The income from this source was shown to be somewhat less than the receipts from tuition fees, and all income was used for the educational enterprise. A two-year course for high-school graduates led to a diploma, a three-year course to a degree of Bachelor of Theatrical Arts, and a four-year course to the degree of Master. The court had no hesitancy in finding that "acting is universally recognized as a profession" and considered the auditorium comparable to a laboratory. The association was held to be "an educational institution of collegiate grade, not conducted for profit, whose profits were being used exclusively for purposes of education."[9]

The Kentucky case is not fully comparable, and affords not a directly contrasting theory but a point of distinction. In denying exemption to a nonstock, nonprofit private club maintaining a playground in Louisville equipped with tennis courts, athletic field, and children's wading pool, at a place where no other playground was available within four miles, and allowing the neighboring public limited access to the facilities, the highest court of the state reversed a lower court judgment that the activity was "not only educational in character, but also educational along lines that are presently important and most neglected." It also took occasion to overrule the forty-year-old decision in *German Gymnastic Association* v. *Louisville* (1904), which had granted exemption on the basis, in part at least, of a schedule of organized class instruction in literary subjects one day each week. Thus a long-standing interpretation of the exemption clause of the Kentucky constitution was expressly rejected. The court reasoned: "While in its broadest and best sense education em-

[9] *Pasadena Playhouse Association* v. *Los Angeles County*, 69 Cal. App. 2d 611, 159 P. 2d 679 (1945).

braces all forms and phases of instruction, improvement and development of mind and body, and as well of religious and moral sentiments, yet in the common understanding and application it means a place where systematic instruction in any or all of the useful branches of learning is given by methods common to schools and institutions of learning. Thus schools for teaching dancing, riding, and other special accomplishments are not schools or institutions of education in the ordinary sense."[10]

A similar attitude toward this type of institution is maintained by the Ohio supreme court, as illustrated by its adverse decision regarding exemption of the plant of a *turnverein* in Cleveland, consisting of a lot and modern brick building equipped with kitchen facilities, rathskeller, dining room, locker rooms, pool and billiard rooms, bowling alleys, and a large gymnasium. The society was a nonprofit corporation having as members about 1,000 men paying dues of $12 a year. Wives and children of members were allowed to use the facilities for small fixed fees. Some children of parents financially unable to join were permitted to participate in the gymnasium classes which constituted the bulk of the program. Having reference to the two sections of the Ohio statutes relevant to the issue, the court, while conceding that the purposes and program of the society were commendable, concluded that it was "neither a '*public* institution of learning' nor an 'institution used *exclusively* for charitable purposes.' "[11]

---

[10] *Kesselring* v. *Bonnycastle Club*, 299 Ky. 585, 186 S.W. 2d 402 (1945).
[11] *Socialer Turnverein* v. *Board of Tax Appeals*, 139 Ohio St. 622, 41 N.E. 2d 710 (1942).

CHAPTER XII
STATE TAXES OTHER THAN THE PROPERTY TAX

CASES have come to the higher courts concerning the obligations of educational institutions with respect to state excise taxes and unemployment compensation taxes, and regarding the application of state succession taxes and estate taxes to transfers of property or funds to charitable corporations.

Excise Tax on Meals Purveyed to the Public

On the question of whether college dormitory dining halls are within the purview of the Massachusetts tax of five per cent on the charges for meals sold in regular public eating places at a price of more than one dollar, Wellesley College asked the attorney general for instructions. When the query reached the Supreme Judicial Court, it was explained that it was not a proper subject for a petition by trustees for instruction, because the answer could have no relevancy to the preservation and execution of the charitable trust:

> The tax, if imposed, is not a charge upon or payable out of trust funds. The amount of the tax is paid by the purchaser of the food, and, if the petitioner is liable for the tax, the fact that it is required to collect and forward the tax to the commissioner would not be sufficient ground upon which it could base an exemption from the tax even though it may incur additional expense in keeping records and filing returns.

Nevertheless the court consented to answer the question to allay confusion promptly, and found no difficulty in declaring that the college, in providing meals exclusively for its own students and faculty and their occasional guests, and for a few temporary summer tenants of apartment dormitories, was not engaged in the business of operating a public eating place, after the manner of restaurants, hotels, and resorts as contemplated in the statute. The college's food service was incidental, though necessary, to its educational function, and in no sense amounted to a business of serving meals to the public. The college was not under obligation to collect and forward the tax, solely because it was not engaging in the activities intended to be taxed.[1] This

---

[1] *Wellesley College* v. *Attorney General*, 313 Mass. 722, 49 N.E. 2d 220 (1943).

was not a matter of exemption from taxation, but instead a case wherein the tax law simply did not apply.

UNEMPLOYMENT COMPENSATION TAXES

In nearly all states, if there is any distribution of property or profits from the operation of the institution to private individuals, the privilege of tax exemption is thereby wholly defeated. Decisions of 1945 in two New England states gave a liberal answer to the further question whether (1) the exemption must depend upon an express prohibition of private gains in the charter, or (2) it can depend on a showing that no distribution was made during the period in dispute and none is contemplated.

The Arnold College for Hygiene and Physical Education was made a nonstock corporation exclusively for educational purposes by a Connecticut special act of 1929 which did not forbid the division of net earnings among individual members. When it sought exemption from the unemployment compensation tax for 1937, the administrator of unemployment compensation ruled against it, holding that the corporation was not nonprofit, though actually the record of eight years of operation showed no permanent balance of profits over losses, and no earnings had been paid to individuals except in reasonable compensation for services rendered. In 1941 the legislature enacted an amendment to the college charter expressly making it nonprofit; but the corporation neglected formally to accept this act by filing a copy of a vote of acceptance with the Secretary of State, as required by a pertinent statute. On this state of facts, a court of first instance rendered judgment against the college; but the highest court of the state set aside that judgment and directed that the exemption be granted.[2]

One judge dissented, maintaining that where the charter is silent as to private gains, then as a matter of law any profits inure to the private benefit of members of the corporation. This theory, rejected by the majority of the Connecticut court, was also denied by the highest court of Massachusetts in the World Wide Broadcasting Foundation case, already discussed in Chapter X.

In New Jersey exemption from the unemployment compensation tax was refused to Consumers' Research, Inc., a nonprofit

[2] *Arnold College for Hygiene and Physical Education* v. *Danaher*, 131 Conn. 503, 41 A. 2d 89 (1945).

corporation engaged in distributing information to prospective purchasers of commercially advertised products. The organization had five members and some 60,000 paying subscribers, had acquired a considerable plant and a modest cash surplus, and paid its own operating expenses, chiefly out of its own earnings. The court remarked that in the event of dissolution of the corporation its assets would be divided among the five members, and therefore decided that it was not in a position such that its net earnings could not "inure to the benefit of any private shareholder or individual" in the words of the exemption statute. Moreover, it was adjudged not to be *exclusively* engaged in scientific and educational work, as required for exemption.[3]

STATE SUCCESSION AND ESTATE TAXES

In Connecticut the executors of a large estate, bound by the will of the testatrix to use their discretion in accomplishing distribution of a large residue to benevolent and charitable institutions, a long list of which was suggested, including the "Fund for Near East Colleges," asked the court for permission to organize a corporation to effect the distribution, and further queried whether the transfer of the residue to such corporation would be subject to succession and estate taxes. It was decided that the plan to create a corporation was too far afield from the wishes of the testatrix as expressed in the will; therefore the tax question need not be answered. It was also decided on appeal that the trial court had erred in holding that all gifts made by the executors during 1939 were for charitable purposes, on no evidence other than the mere statement of one of the executors to that effect. This means that the charitable character of transfers must be determined upon a thorough examination of evidence, and not lightly upon unverified testimony.[4]

DEDUCTION OF BEQUESTS TO FOREIGN CORPORATIONS

A North Dakota testator made bequests to the National Jewish Hospital, the Methodist Episcopal Board of Foreign Missions, and the "Michigan University Religious Association,"

---

[3] *Consumers' Research, Inc., et al.* v. *Evans*, 128 N.J.L. 95, 24 A. 2d 390 (1942); affirmed without opinion, 132 N.J.L. 431, 40 A. 2d 662 (1945).

[4] *Cochran et al.* v. *McLaughlin, Tax Commissioner, et al.*, 128 Conn. 638, 24 A. 2d 836 (1942).

all of which were corporations foreign to North Dakota. The bequests were deductible from the estate for purposes of the North Dakota estate tax. In the words of Chief Justice Burr:[5]

> The language of our statute is quite plain. It permits the administrator to deduct from the gross value of the estate 'the amount of all bequests ... for any charitable, educational, or religious purpose. ...' It makes no pretense to limit the place of this work. It does not confine the locality to this State. The philanthropic interests of American citizens have never been confined within geographical limitations. In innumerable instances the State has been the beneficiary of such bequests from outside sources, and the citizens of the State have been liberal in making similar donations.

When Are Deductible Charitable Legacies Charged with a Share of the Tax on the Net Estate?

Bearing in mind that an estate tax is levied on the privilege of transferring the entire net estate, and not on the transfer of separate legacies, one easily discerns that in addition to the question of the deductibility of charitable bequests from the gross estate, there is also the quite different question of whether charitable legacies shall be proportionally reduced by being charged with their share of the tax on the net estate. The Florida supreme court, on a petition for instruction on this point from the executor of an estate, with reference to the federal and state estate taxes, gave an affirmative answer. Under federal and Florida law the testator could have stipulated that the charitable bequest should be exempt from its share of the tax on the net estate; but in the absence of such a stipulation, the charitable bequest is presumed to have been intended to be set aside in like manner as other bequests and to bear its portion of estate taxes and other expenses of administration.[6]

---

[5] *In re McKee's Estate; Melby* v. *State et al.,* 71 N.D. 545, 3 N.W. 2d 797 (1942).
[6] *In re Bernays' Estate; Art Students' League of New York, Inc.,* v. *Wislocki,* (Fla.), 7 So. 2d 444 (1942).

CHAPTER XIII
THE FEDERAL ESTATE TAX

THE Federal Revenue Act allows the deduction from the gross estate of legacies to nonprofit educational and charitable institutions, before the federal estate tax is computed. The recent cases have been concerned, for the most part, with two types of questions: (1) whether the intended charitable legatee devotes a substantial portion of its activities to influencing legislation, and therefore promotes political rather than charitable purposes; and (2) whether the bequest to charity is certain or contingent.

ACTIVITIES OF CHARITABLE LEGATEE IN ATTEMPTING TO INFLUENCE LEGISLATION

One of the most interesting decisions of the period concerned the deduction of a bequest to the Board of Temperance, Prohibition and Public Morals of the Methodist Episcopal Church. The issue was whether the lobbying activities of that organization should disqualify it as a charitable legatee. The Board of Tax Appeals disallowed the deduction, but the decision was reversed by a divided vote of the United States Circuit Court of Appeals. In the majority opinion, Circuit Judge Goodrich, elucidating the definition of a charitable trust, pointed out that "the object of the trust does not have to be the advancement of a majority view. It must not, of course, call for violation of law nor must it be 'irrational.' It is only when the court is convinced that the purpose of the trust can serve no rational object that the court will declare it invalid." He also quoted from Circuit Judge Learned Hand in a 1930 decision wherein that distinguished jurist, after declaring that political agitation or propaganda is not a charitable purpose eligible for tax exemption, went on to say:

Nevertheless, there are many charitable, literary and scientific ventures that as an incident to their success require changes in the law. A charity may need a special charter allowing it to receive larger gifts than the general laws allow. It would be strained to say that for this reason it became less exclusively charitable, though much might have to be done to convince legislators. . . . A state university is constantly trying to get appropriations from the legislature; for all that, it seems to us still an exclusively educational institution. No less so if, for instance, in Tennessee it tries to get leave to teach evolutionary biology.

Circuit Judge Clark entered a dissenting opinion in which he agreed that the wisdom or popularity of the particular cause for which money is given is no concern of the courts, but asserted preference for the view which has always been maintained by the courts of England and of Massachusetts, to the effect that a trust is not charitable if the attainment of its purpose involves a change in existing law. In explication of this view he quoted from a 1917 decision of Lord Parker:

> A trust for the attainment of political objects has always been held invalid, not because it is illegal, for everyone is at liberty to advocate or promote by any lawful means a change in the law, but because the court has no means of judging whether a proposed change in the law will or will not be for the public benefit, and therefore cannot say that a gift to secure the change is a charitable gift.

Concluding his dissent with a pointed thrust, Judge Clark said, "Undoubtedly there is a faint odor of harm in the use of money to present only one side of any proposition. To paraphrase, it may place the Lord on the side of the heaviest moneybags [reference to Voltaire]. Although, therefore, one may not object, he may assuredly refrain from encouraging—either by way of offering the state's help in enforcement or in subvention."[1]

GIFTS FOR POLITICAL PURPOSES NOT DEDUCTIBLE

Four years later the same court decided against the deduction of a bequest to the United Committee for the Taxation of Land Values, Limited, an English corporation largely engaged in carrying on political propaganda and attempting to influence legislation. In this case the testator was a New Jersey resident who had long been greatly interested in the single tax doctrines of Henry George, and the bequest was made obviously to support and advance those doctrines. Circuit Judge Goodrich distinguished the case from the Methodist Board case by pointing out that here there was no evidence of any religious purpose. Moreover, the pertinent exemption clause of the Federal Rev-

[1] *Girard Trust Co. et al.* v. *Collector of Internal Revenue*, (U.S.C.C.A.), 122 F. 2d 108, 138 A.L.R. 448 (1941).

enue Act had been slightly amended since the former decision.[2]

The same principles were involved in another decision denying deduction of sums bequeathed by Robert Marshall of New York City to establish three trusts. The purpose of one of these was to educate the people of the United States to the necessity and desirability of labor organizations for workers and the unemployed, and of an economic system based on the theory of production for use and not for profit. The second trust was for the safeguarding and advancement of civil liberties, and the third was for the preservation of wilderness conditions in outdoor America. All three trusts were to operate only by lawful means, and were authorized to hire organizers, lecturers, and writers, and to draft bills and use all lawful means to obtain their enactment. In denying the deduction, the court said: "The objects aimed at in all three trusts are to a substantial extent political, however desirable the politics may be thought to be by some." And, "however lawful such a means is, it will necessarily involve political agitation which 'must be conducted without public subvention.' "[3]

PREFERENCE FOR RELATIVES AS CHARITABLE BENEFICIARIES DOES NOT DEFEAT DEDUCTION

Charles Gulentz of Pittsburgh, who died in 1941, bequeathed $100,000 to the Carnegie Institute of Technology in trust to provide tuition scholarships, and a residuary legacy of about $135,000 to Georgetown University to provide scholarships covering tuition, board, and lodging. In both instances the scholarships were to be of two classes, the first class being for a limited number of eligible persons of the name of Gulentz who were in any way related to the testator's family, limited to high-school graduates who were sound physically and in need of help. The second class of scholarships was for eligible persons of the Roman Catholic faith and of good moral character. The will stipulated that if in any year there were no applicants of the first class, then the fund should be available for that year to applicants of the second class; and if in any year there were no applicants of

[2] *Sharpe's Estate* v. *Collector of Internal Revenue*, (U.S.C.C.A.), 148 F. 2d 179 (1945).
[3] *Marshall* v. *Collector of Internal Revenue*, (U.S.C.C.A.), 147 F. 2d 75 (1945). Certiorari denied, 325 U.S. 872, 65 S. Ct. 1413, 90 L. Ed. 63 (1945); and rehearing denied, 326 U.S. 804, 66 S. Ct. 14, 89 L. Ed. 1991 (1945).

either class, then the fund should be available for that year to non-Catholic applicants.

The Collector of Internal Revenue ruled that in each bequest the provision for scholarships for the testator's relatives was not charitable, and assessed the estate tax against a sufficient portion of each bequest to capitalize the designated scholarships at four per cent. This ruling was not sustained in the federal District Court, where the estate was allowed to recover the amount of the deficiency assessment. It was held that both bequests were wholly charitable, because the will indicated no more than a preference for relatives of the testator as charitable beneficiaries, and not a limitation to that class.[4]

Certainty Is Essential to Deductibility

The familiar principle that a testamentary gift which is contingent and not certain cannot be deducted for purposes of the federal estate tax was again illustrated. A decedent who left bequests aggregating some $400,000 to such educational institution as might be selected within one year by his sister and his nephew stipulated in his will that, if no such selections were made within the year, then the legacy should lapse and be added to his residuary estate. The case was clearly covered by Treasury Regulation No. 80, to the effect that "if a gift may be diverted in whole or in part by the exercise of a power . . . the deduction will be limited to that portion, if any, of the property or fund which is exempt from an exercise of such power." Consequently the federal court concluded that the bequests were "too uncertain to make them deductible within the provisions of the statute."[5]

An equally clear case was that of the will of Frank B. Kellogg, former Secretary of State of the United States, who died in 1937, making certain specific bequests to charitable institutions, with his wife, Clara M. Kellogg, an unconditional beneficiary of the residuary estate. One of the specific bequests was of $25,000 to the University of Minnesota; but its validity was expressly conditioned upon the written assent of Clara M. Kellogg, given between the date of the testator's death and the date set by the pro-

---

[4] *Commonwealth Trust Co.* v. *Granger*, (U.S.D.C.), 57 F. Supp. 502 (1944).

[5] *Burdick* v. *Collector of Internal Revenue*, (U.S.C.C.A.), 117 F. 2d 972 (1941). Certiorari denied, 314 U.S. 631, 62 S. Ct. 63, 86 L. Ed. 506 (1941).

bate court for hearing on the final account and distribution of the estate. Mrs. Kellogg in fact filed her written assent, whereupon the executors paid the bequest to the University of Minnesota and deducted the amount from the gross estate in their federal estate tax return. The deduction was disallowed, because when a will contains no mandatory requirement that anything shall pass from the estate to any charitable institution, the contingent or conditional bequest lacks the legal certainty necessary to make it deductible.[6]

Somewhat similar was the case of a Wisconsin testatrix who placed her estate in the hands of two trustees and authorized them to select and designate charitable legatees and determine the amounts each should receive. The trustees in fact gave $5,000 to the Columbia Hospital in Milwaukee, and $284,341.10 to the Norris Foundation, a Wisconsin charitable corporation. Deduction of these amounts for federal estate tax purposes was not allowed, because under the terms of the will the gifts were "at the discretion and option" of the trustees, and apparently the will did not actually make mandatory any charitable bequest at all.[7]

ACTUARIAL ASCERTAINMENT OF VALUE OF CHARITABLE BEQUEST

It appears that if the value of a bequest to charity is actually determinable at the time of the testator's death, the deduction of the actuarial value will be allowed, even though there is a possibility that in the course of human events the bequest may be defeated altogether. Thus a testator died in 1937, setting up a $30,000 trust, with the income thereof to his sister (aged 74) for life. If at her death her husband (aged 79) should not be living, the corpus would go to the decedent's widow (aged 71); and if she were not living, to Columbia University. On the other hand, if at the death of the sister her husband should be living, then one-half of the corpus should be held in trust for him for life, and on his death go to decedent's wife if living, or if not living, to Columbia University; the other half to go at the sister's death

---

[6] *First Trust Co. of St. Paul State Bank* v. *Reynolds, Collector of Internal Revenue*, (U.S. C.C.A.), 137 F. 2d 518 (1943), affirming *Same*, (U.S.D.C.), 46 F. Supp. 497 (1942).

[7] *Norris et al.* v. *Collector of Internal Revenue*, (U.S.C.C.A.), 134 F. 2d 796 (1943); certiorari denied, 320 U.S. 756, 64 S. Ct. 63, 88 L. Ed. 450 (1943); petition for rehearing denied, 320 U.S. 813, 64 S. Ct. 199, 88 L. Ed. 491 (1943).

to decedent's wife if living, or if not, to Columbia University.

Observe that if decedent's wife should survive both the sister and the sister's husband, Columbia University would take nothing; but that the contingency depended not upon anyone's discretion or volition—its likelihood was precisely ascertainable by methods in customary use by actuaries. The actuarially computed value of Columbia University's interest in the estate at the time of the testator's death was $9,836.70, and accordingly it was held that this amount should have been deducted from the gross estate for tax purposes, and recovery for the corresponding overpayment was allowed.[8]

The same principle was followed in a 1945 decision regarding a testamentary trust for the benefit of two named persons (aged respectively 60 and 64 at the inception of the trust) during their lives, after which the principal would go to a third person (aged 84) if then living; or, if not living, to named charitable organizations. The United States District Court quoted and followed the holding that the right to deduct in a case of this type "depends not on whether the bequest is contingent or vested, but on whether it has an ascertainable market value," and decided that the actuarially determined value of the contingent charitable bequests at the time of the testatrix's death should have been deducted. In this instance the amount deductible was $90,450.60, in consequence of which the estate was allowed to recover $13,-375.82 as overpaid estate tax.[9]

Trust for Private Beneficiary for Life, with Power to Invade Corpus, and Remainder to Charity

During the past five years an unusual number of cases has furnished the federal courts a forest in which to blaze a boundary line indicating the limit of permissible contingencies beyond which a charitable bequest is not deductible for tax purposes.

In one instance a testator left his estate in trust, directing the trustees to pay to his widow "the income thereof and so much of the principal as she may need or desire during her life," the remainder to go to designated charitable legatees, chief among which was the Grenfell Association. At the time of his death the

---

[8] *Meierhof* v. *Higgins, Collector of Internal Revenue,* (U.S.C.C.A.), 129 F. 2d 1002 (1942).
[9] *Gardiner et al.* v. *Hassett,* (U.S.D.C.), 63 F. Supp. 853 (1945).

widow was 93 years of age, an invalid, and possessed property worth about $190,000 in her own right. The court held that the charitable bequests were not deductible, because their value was not definitely ascertainable at the date of the testator's death. He intended, thought the court, to give his widow "a broad power of invasion of the principal, not restricted to a mere use of the corpus for the purpose of satisfying her needs."[10]

A similar result was reached in another case where the widow was wealthy in her own right, and the trustee of her late husband's estate was to pay her the net income for life, and was also authorized to pay her "such sum or sums from the principal of the trust fund and at such time or times as my said Trustee shall in its sole discretion deem wise and proper for the comfort, support, maintenance and/or happiness of my said wife." The will further directed the trustee to exercise the granted discretion "with liberality." The case reached the United States Supreme Court, where the opinion was written by Mr. Justice Rutledge, with Justices Douglas and Jackson dissenting. The opinion of the court points out that Treasury Regulations provide that

> where a trust is created for both charitable and private purposes, the charitable bequest, to be deductible, must have, at the testator's death, a value 'presently ascertainable, and hence severable from the interest in favor of the private use,' and further, to the extent that there is power in a private donee or trustee to divert the property from the charity, 'deduction will be limited to that portion, if any, of the property or fund which is exempt from an exercise of such power.'

Applying the principle to the present case, the court concluded:[11]

> Introducing the element of the widow's happiness and instructing the trustee to exercise its discretion with liberality to make her wishes prior to the claims of residuary beneficiaries brought into the calculation elements of speculation too large to be overcome, notwithstanding the widow's previous mode of life was modest and her own resources substantial.

The same principles were applied in the decision of a more

---

[10] *Gammons* v. *Hassett*, (U.S.C.C.A.), 121 F. 2d 229 (1941); certiorari denied, 314 U.S. 673, 62 S. Ct. 136, 86 L. Ed. 539 (1941).

[11] *Merchants' National Bank of Boston* v. *Collector of Internal Revenue*, 320 U.S. 256, 64 S. Ct. 108, 88 L. Ed. 35 (1943). Affirms (U.S.C.C.A.), 132 F. 2d 483 (1942), from which certiorari was granted, 319 U.S. 734, 63 S. Ct. 1031, 87 L. Ed. 1695 (1943).

recent case wherein a testator who died in Providence in 1938 left provisions for the care of his wife (aged 65), his mother (who died in 1941), and his sister (who died in 1945). A claimed deduction of $1,326,000 from the gross estate of $1,873,000 was disallowed. The will directed the trustees to pay an annuity of $12,000 to the wife, and $6,000 each to the mother and sister during their respective lives. It also authorized the trustees to pay to these beneficiaries "so much of the net income of the trust, or if that be insufficient, so much of the principal as the trustees deem proper for the comfort and pleasure" of the individual beneficiary in each case, in their "sole and uncontrolled discretion." It further directed that "said powers and discretion be liberally construed for the benefit of my wife for the assurance of her comfortable maintenance and support." The chief charitable remainderman was the Rhode Island Hospital. The disallowance of deduction was affirmed on principle, and the fact that during the period 1939–42 the income of the trust was substantially greater than the total of outpayments was not deemed to affect the issue.[12]

WHERE THE PROBABILITY OF INVASION OF THE CORPUS IS "SO REMOTE AS TO BE NEGLIGIBLE"

Another train of federal decisions is on the other side of the line, stemming from the Bonfils Trust case discussed at pages 72 and 73 of *The Colleges and the Courts*, 1936–40 (predecessor of this volume), and the famous case of *Ithaca Trust Co.* v. *United States*, 279 U.S. 151, 49 S. Ct. 291, 73 L. Ed. 647 (1929), wherein the claimed deductions were allowed.

In one case a testator leaving a gross estate of $114,000 provided life payments of $250 a month for his sister, "and in case she should, by reason of accident, illness, or other unusual circumstances so require, such additional sum or sums as in the judgment of said trustee may be necessary and reasonable under the existing conditions." At her death the trust was to be liquidated and paid over to named charities. The sister was aged 79 and nearly blind. She owned a $3,500 home, bank accounts aggregating $7,400, and $16,000 in stocks and bonds. Her an-

---

12 *Industrial Trust Co. et al.* v. *Collector of Internal Revenue*, (U.S.C.C.A.), 151 F. 2d 592 (1945). Certiorari denied, 66 S. Ct. 530, 90 L. Ed. 466 (1946).

nual income was about $900, and her living expenses about $1,450. During the period 1937–40 the annual income of the trust set up by her deceased brother was always in excess of the $3,000 allowance provided for her. The court concluded that the "probability of an invasion of the corpus was remote indeed," and decided that the bequests to the charities were sufficiently ascertainable to be deducted.[13]

In another instance a testatrix disposing of a $200,000 estate placed a large residue in trust, with income to her aged sister for life, and thereafter the entire remainder to designated charities. Further, said the will, "My said trustee is authorized to pay to my said sister . . . any portion of the principal sum . . . if in the judgment of the said trustee, the best interests of my sister should so require." The sister had an estate of her own worth $150,000, and lived frugally with her aged husband at a cost of about $3,000 a year. Her annual income from her own resources was about $4,200 a year, and she had a consistent record of substantial savings each year for several recent years. In these circumstances the United States Tax Court held that "the possibility of invasion of the corpus is so remote as to be nil." The Circuit Court of Appeals, affirming the judgment in favor of deduction of the trust fund as definitely set aside for charitable purposes, declared: "To hold otherwise would not only invade the province of the Tax Court but frustrate the obvious intent of Congress to encourage charitable bequests by allowing corresponding deductions from the taxable estate."[14]

Very similar were the facts and the reasoning in a contemporaneous case wherein a testatrix who died in 1940 left a residuary estate of $130,000 in trust, with income to her niece for life and corpus to charity thereafter. The trustees were empowered to apply such part of the principal as they deemed reasonable to assist the niece in case of her need "on account of any sickness, accident, want, or other emergency." The niece had about $35,000 in her own right. She died in 1942. The income of the trust was $4,000 a year, and the trustees paid her $300 a month while she lived, and held the surplus $400 a year in trust for her. Apparently the court took some notice of the actual

---

[13] *Collector of Internal Revenue* v. *Bank of America National Trust and Savings Association*, (U.S.C.C.A.), 133 F. 2d 753 (1943).

[14] *Collector of Internal Revenue* v. *Robertson's Estate*, (U.S.C.C.A.), 141 F. 2d 855 (1944).

course of events subsequent to the testatrix's death to support its conclusion that the charitable remainder was definitely ascertainable at the time of her death, and therefore deductible for estate-tax purposes.[15]

But the principle that the value must be determinable from data available at the death of the decedent was forcefully emphasized in another case where a man who was already trustee of a fund producing $7,000 income annually for his sister, created another *inter vivos* trust from which she was to receive the income for life plus authority to invade the principal up to 10 per cent thereof each year, in case of emergency. The remainder was to go to charity. At the time of his death in 1940 his sister was 60 years old, in good health, and of thrifty habit. She was regularly saving about half of her $7,000 annual income from the first trust. The evidence tended to indicate that there would be only extremely remote likelihood that she would use any part of the principal of the second trust. In fact, however, it turned out that she did invade the principal shortly after her brother's death, because her income from both trusts was suspended pending settlement of a legal controversy. In this situation the Tax Court intimated that it would have held the principal deductible as a gift to charity on the basis of the facts as they stood at the death of the brother, but that it must hold otherwise in the face of the fact that the principal had actually been invaded. The Circuit Court of Appeals was quick to reverse and remand the decision, in an opinion adhering to the rule that the determination must be as of the date of the decedent's death, and unaffected by the subsequent course of events.[16]

WHERE CHARITABLE BEQUESTS ARE REDUCED BY THE TAX ON THE ESTATE THE AMOUNT DEDUCTIBLE IS ONLY THE AMOUNT ACTUALLY DISTRIBUTED TO CHARITABLE DONEES

In 1943 the Supreme Court of the United States reviewed the case of an Illinois testator whose net residuary estate bequeathed to charitable legatees amounted to $463,103.08, but under the will was charged with payment of $459,879.57 of

15 *Collector of Internal Revenue* v. *Wells-Fargo Bank and Union Trust Co.,* (U.S.C.C.A.), 145 F. 2d 130 (1944).
16 *Wells-Fargo Bank and Union Trust Co.* v. *Collector of Internal Revenue,* (U.S.C.C.A.), 145 F. 2d 132 (1944).

the federal estate tax on the entire large estate, leaving only $3,223.51 actually to pass to the residuary legatees. The question whether in these circumstances the amount deductible should be the actual amount of the bequests, after payment of federal income taxes, or what would have been the amount if there had been no such taxes, was decided in favor of the Government on the strength of Section 807 of the Revenue Act of 1932, which so provided, but in language not completely unambiguous. Mr. Justice Murphy, for the unanimous court, pointed out from the legislative history of the section that it was unquestionably enacted to effect a legislative reversal of the contrary decision on the same point in *Edwards* v. *Slocum*, 264 U.S. 61, 44 S. Ct. 293, 68 L. Ed. 564 (1924), and this left no doubt of the intent of Congress.[17]

---

[17] *Harrison* v. *Northern Trust Company et al.*, 317 U.S. 476, 63 S. Ct. 361, 87 L. Ed. 407 (1943); reversing *Same*, (U.S.C.C.A.), 125 F. 2d 893 (1942), from which certiorari was granted, 317 U.S. 612, 63 S. Ct. 29, 87 L. Ed. 497 (1942).

CHAPTER XIV
FEDERAL TAXES OTHER THAN THE ESTATE TAX

HERE appear cases concerning the deduction of gifts to charitable and educational institutions from the donor's taxable income under the federal income tax; what parts of the income of certain testamentary trusts may be adjudged to be permanently set aside for the charitable remaindermen and thus deductible in the income tax returns; the exemption of a corporation for civic, educational, and cultural purposes from liability for the federal excess profits tax; the exemption of an educational institution from the federal social security tax; and an attempt by a commercial concern to escape the federal income tax on corporations on the ground that its stock was wholly owned by a state university.

Federal Tax on Individual Incomes

The decision in *Schoellkopf* v. *United States*, discussed at pages 71 and 72 of *The Colleges and the Courts* 1936–40, was carried up on appeal and affirmed in 1942. The federal district court's holding that "the gift of the Boston Trust was a charitable gift, no part of which could be recaptured by the grantor and no part of the income of which inured to the benefit of the grantor or any private individual" was correct, and its charitable character was not affected, said the Circuit Court of Appeals, by the fact that eventually certain gifts for charitable purposes were to be made out of the trust funds to two cities in Württemberg, Germany; nor by the fact that the ultimate trustee was instructed that worthy descendants of the donor's father might be included among the charitable beneficiaries, without limiting the benefits to that class of persons, nor even directing a preference for them.[1]

Capital Gains Accruing to Testamentary Trust Eventually Destined for Charity

At the death of Edwin Ginn in 1914 his testamentary trust came into being, providing for life annuities for numerous mem-

---

[1] *Schoellkopf* v. *United States*, (U.S.C.C.A.), 124 F. 2d 982 (1942), affirming *Same*, 36 F. Supp. 617 (1941).

bers of his family, and an annuity not to exceed $40,000 for the
World Peace Foundation, and ultimate disposition of the corpus of some $1,800,000 in such manner that twenty-nine thirti-
eths of it would go to charitable institutions among which was
Tufts College, and one-thirtieth to a natural person. During
the years 1931, 1932, and 1934 the trust fund gained substantially from two sources: (1) surplus income, over and above all
payments to the designated annuitants; and (2) capital gains re-
sulting from net profits from sales of real estate, stocks, and bonds.
The accretions of both types were taxed as income, and the trustees sued to recover on the ground that these items should be
exempt as permanently set aside for charitable purposes. The
court decided, after the manner of the Bonfils Trust case of 1940,
that under the circumstances there was no likelihood that the
corpus of the trust would be invaded to meet the obligations to
private beneficiaries, and therefore the capital gains would be
properly regarded as accretions to a charitable fund. Accordingly the trustees were allowed to recover the income taxes paid
on twenty-nine thirtieths of the capital gains during the years in
dispute.[2]

As to the surplus income for the same years, the decision was
that it did not become a part of the corpus, but was subject to
invasion to supply possible deficiencies in future years, and was
therefore properly taxable as income of the private trust.

On this point, another federal court went further in a contemporaneous case wherein the facts favored greater liberality. Here
a testator who died in 1932 left a testamentary trust corpus of
some $2,500,000, of which the reasonably predictable income
was from three to four times the obligations of the trust to private persons. Under these circumstances it was held that the annual income which was surplus over the outpayments was deductible from the gross income for tax purposes, as permanently
set aside for charitable purposes.[3] The same decision also declared that the charitable and tax-exempt character of the ultimate trust was not destroyed or impaired by the fact that the
trustee was given full discretion to choose the charitable and
"public welfare" beneficiaries; and the use of the adjective

[2] *Holcombe et al.* v. *United States*, (U.S.D.C.), 41 F. Supp. 471 (1941).
[3] *Collector of Internal Revenue* v. *Upjohn's Estate*, (U.S.C.C.A.), 124 F. 2d 73 (1941).

phrase "public welfare" did not create a possibility of noncharitable expenditure, because it is synonymous with "charitable" in the public mind.

Related decisions of federal courts on when the corpus of a trust set up for both private and charitable purposes is properly regarded as a permanently dedicated charitable fund appear in Chapter XIII; and decisions of state and federal courts on the requisites to the validity of charitable trusts are discussed in Chapters XVI and XVII.

FEDERAL EXCESS PROFITS TAX

The Debs Memorial Radio Fund, Inc., is a corporation organized in 1928 under the New York Stock Corporation Law. In 1932 its bylaw providing for distribution of dividends was repealed and superseded by one directing that all profits be used either for the improvement of its radio broadcasting facilities or for "civic, educational, and cultural purposes." Its sole activity has been the ownership and operation of Station WEVD for radio broadcasting. It sells considerable commercial radio time as a means of obtaining funds to sustain its non-commercial program. During most of the years up to 1940 it operated with annual deficits. Its net income for that year was about $30,000, but at the end of the year the aggregate of expenses of operation still exceeded the total of receipts by some $37,000. At various times it had received advances of substantial funds from the Forward Association, a New York corporation interested in the advancement of similar civic ideas; and its shares of stock are now all held by individuals nominated by the Forward Association.

By determination of the revenue collector and the United States Tax Court a deficiency assessment for federal excess profits tax for the year 1940 was made against the Debs Memorial Radio Fund, Inc., but this determination was reversed by the Circuit Court of Appeals, holding that the corporation is properly within the meaning of that section of the applicable Federal Revenue Act which provides for the exemption of "civic leagues or organizations not organized for profit but operated exclusively for ... social welfare. ..." The opinion by Circuit Judge Swan pointed out that in fact no person or corporation derives private profit from the enterprise, and its nonprofit character is not destroyed by the conduct of commercial broadcasting for the purpose of using the proceeds to enable it to broadcast free educational and civic programs.[4]

Circuit Judge Chase dissented, believing "exemption statutes should be strictly construed," and that the Circuit Court of Appeals should not overturn administrative determinations where they are supported by substantial evidence—with reference in this case to the facts in the record indicating that a part of the income of the organization was used to expand its commercial activities, as well as to support directly its non-commercial function. Nowhere is any question raised as to the bearing, if any, of the fact that the social theories and civic ideas of Eugene V. Debs and of the Forward Association were substantially those of an organized political party. Here we are concerned with the federal excess profits tax assessed against a nonprofit corporation, and not with a bequest to such a corporation and its possible deduction from the testator's estate for purposes of the federal estate tax; but comparison with the first three cases discussed in the preceding chapter is suggested.

FEDERAL SOCIAL SECURITY TAX

In New York City federal social security taxes against a Czechoslovakian gymnastic association as an employer of persons in allegedly covered occupations were collected in the amount of $47.87, but the association was allowed to recover the amount by a decision holding that it was a corporation organized exclusively for educational purposes, no part of the net earnings of which accrued to the benefit of any shareholder or individual.

The organization owned a building on East 71st Street, containing a large gymnasium, music room, library, kitchen, restaurant, bar, and bowling alleys. It maintained regular daily schedules of gymnastic instruction for persons of different ages and sexes, and classes in choral singing. More than 90 per cent of its gross annual receipts came from the bar and restaurant, and nearly all income from that source was paid out for food, wages of employees, and other operating expenses. The collector contended that it was a "mere social club"; but Circuit Judge Augustus N. Hand, speaking for the court, concluded that the me-

[4] *Debs Memorial Radio Fund, Inc.,* v. *Collector of Internal Revenue,* (U.S.C.C.A.), 148 F. 2d 948 (1945).

thodical instruction in physical and cultural development and the continuous pursuit of those objects are properly regarded as educational.[5]

Less liberal treatment of a similar institution by a state court under state tax laws has been observed in the *Socialer Turnverein* case in Chapter XI.

CORPORATION INCOME TAX ON INCORPORATED BUSINESS WHOLLY OWNED BY A STATE UNIVERSITY

The peculiar spectacle of an ordinary business corporation seeking exemption from the federal tax on corporation incomes, on the ground that its stock was all owned by the University of California, occurred in 1941. The university had in fact been the sole stockholder since about 1920 in a waterworks company in San Mateo County, which sold its service to private consumers and did not serve the university at all. The company claimed federal tax exemption for the years 1933 and 1934, alleging that it was "a corporation exclusively for educational purposes" and that its income was "derived from a public utility and accruing to a State or political subdivision of a State" within the language of the Federal Revenue Act. An adverse decision was affirmed by the Circuit Court of Appeals on elementary principles: The company was a business corporation organized and operated for profit, and there was no evidence that it had been merged with, or become an *alter ego* of, the university corporation. A corporation is an entity quite distinct from the identity of its stockholders.[6]

[5] *Bohemian Gymnastic Association Sokol of City of New York* v. *Higgins,* (U.S.C.C.A.), 147 F. 2d 774 (1945).
[6] *Bear Gulch Water Company* v. *Collector of Internal Revenue,* (U.S.C.C.A.), 116 F. 2d 975 (1941). Certiorari denied, 314 U.S. 652, 62 S. Ct. 99, 86 L. Ed. 523 (1941).

PART FIVE

Financial Support from Private Sources; Institutional Property; Other Matters

∴

CHAPTER XV
THE VALIDITY OF SUBSCRIPTIONS

A SUBSCRIPTION to a school or college, though often popularly thought of as only a promise of a gift, must actually be a contract if it is to be legally irrevocable during the subscriber's life and enforceable against his estate after his death. The courts frequently have to decide questions relating either to the validity of the subscription as a contract, or, if its validity is unquestioned, to the performance of the stipulated conditions by the parties.

When Is a Subscription a Valid Contract?

The disputed issue is usually whether there is a "consideration" (technically defined as "some benefit to the promisor or detriment to the promisee, inducing the promise"), or whether the subscription is merely an unsupported promise revocable by the subscriber and incapable of surviving him. Through two centuries the courts have generally favored the enforcement of *bona fide* subscriptions, and three distinct theories of "consideration" have been evolved: (1) The doctrine that a contract is created when the institution takes a step in reliance on the subscription, such as beginning the construction of a building; (2) the theory that the promises of several subscribers to the same enterprise constitute a "consideration" each for the others; and (3) the doctrine that the general benefit to the community which the subscriber must have contemplated is a sufficient consideration.

The Doctrine of Promissory Estoppel

Two cases of 1940–41 strongly sustain the tendency to find grounds upon which to enforce subscriptions to educational institutions. That a charitable subscription becomes binding and

irrevocable as soon as the beneficiary institution has actually ex-
pended money or incurred obligations in reliance upon it, is the
principle upon which the Missouri supreme court held enforceable a subscription of $10,000 made in 1918 by a husband and
wife, payable to Missouri Wesleyan College at the death of the
surviving spouse. This contingency did not occur until 1934,
four years after the college had closed its doors and effected a
merger with Baker University. Its board of trustees sued on the
instrument and showed that the college had operated for twelve
years after the subscription was made and had spent money and
incurred debts in reliance upon it and others of like tenor. In this
situation, thought the court, the obligation must be regarded as
irrevocable. Hence an attempted revocation by the surviving
widow a few months before her death was of no effect. Nor was
the court concerned that the sum subscribed would apparently
be used to pay off debts of the institution which was no longer
operating. The subscription instrument had recited on its face
that it was "for the purpose of providing one-half million pro-
ductive endowment, and paying all indebtedness in behalf of
Missouri Wesleyan College."[1]

A New York court set forth an even stronger doctrine in
sustaining the validity of a subscription in which the signer, now
deceased, agreed to pay to Hillsdale College in Michigan $1,000
for "two memorial windows" in a new library building. At the
time of the suit the building was in process of erection, thus furnishing an excellent opportunity to hold the subscription enforceable under the doctrine of promissory estoppel, as illustrated in the preceding case, but the court went beyond that
theory and declared that the agreement could be said to constitute of itself a bilateral contract in which a promise was given
for a promise; or, under a third view of the transaction, it could
be regarded as a unilateral contract subsequently consummated.
Under either of these theories it would be valid and enforceable.[2]

The Theory of Mutual Subscriptions

The second theory was under scrutiny in three recent cases,
with somewhat equivocal results. A subscriber signed an instru-

[1] *Missouri Wesleyan College* v. *Shulte*, 346 Mo. 628, 142 S.W. 2d 644 (1940).
[2] *In re Lord's Will*, 175 Misc. 921, 25 N.Y.S. 2d 747 (1941).

ment reciting: "In consideration of the contributions and gifts to be made by others to the endowment and equipment funds of Wesleyan University, Middletown, Conn., I hereby agree to give to the trustees of said university, five thousand dollars . . ., which gifts will aggregate eighty-nine thousand dollars. These gifts are to be applied toward the endowment, in the name of Chester D. Hubbard, of the Chair of Economics and Social Science." Seven years after the death of the subscriber his executors gave a demand note for the $43,000 then unpaid. Eventually the university sued the estate on this note, and met defeat in the highest court of West Virginia, by a divided decision.

The majority of the court, speaking through Justice Kenna, adjudged the original subscription to be "only a continuing offer to become legally bound to pay, if and when the trustees procure other pledges." Further, in the words of the court, "Wesleyan University is not shown to have altered its position in the least due to the pledge . . .; it created no Chair of Economics and Social Science, incurred no obligations, suffered no detriment, and parted with nothing."[3]

Vigorous dissent was entered by Justices Rose and Fox, who pointed out that another individual had subscribed $11,000 on the same day, and this had been paid in full. Moreover, free assets in the hands of the executors were believed to be sufficient to pay the Wesleyan claim in full. These two judges argued, to no avail, that the subscriber was not merely offering a gift, but that his intent was to establish a memorial to his father, "a thing personally and peculiarly valuable to Hubbard individually." No doubt, said they, an offer to pay $89,000 for the erection of a statue, if legally accepted, would be a binding contract. Why not the same for a chair of economics?

KENTUCKY CASES

A contemporaneous Kentucky decision is unequivocal. The Scott-Lees Collegiate Institute sued the administrator and heirs-at-law of a subscriber who had signed four promissory notes for $200 each. Justice Fulton disposed of the matter tersely: "It was alleged that the notes were executed as a donation in consideration of the subscription of other donors to a fund of $50,-

---

[3] *Wesleyan University* v. *Hubbard et al.*, 124 W.Va. 434 20 S.E. 2d 677 (1942).

ooo which the Institute agreed to raise and expend in the erection of a dormitory. This was a sufficient consideration."[4] The
court was unanimous.

But the waters of Kentucky law were soon muddied. In the
following year the same court had before it a subscription signed
by man and wife, in these words: "For the purpose of promoting
Christian education, and in consideration of the gifts of others,
the undersigned hereby agrees to pay to Transylvania University, at Lexington, Kentucky, $5,000 payable as follows: 60
days after the death of the survivor of us. Bequests in my will
amounting to $3,400 to our relatives are preferred to this
pledge." The survivor died in 1937, leaving an estate of $21,-
ooo and a will executed a few days before his death, revoking
all previous wills and bequeathing the entire residuary estate to
his brothers and sisters. A lower court rendered judgment for
the university on the subscription, but on appeal this was reversed with direction to dismiss.

Justice Tilford wrote the opinion, holding that the subscription was not supported by valid consideration and was therefore
not a contract. He thought it was "merely an evidence of dona-
tive intent, of the nature of a testamentary disposition revocable
before death." In this opinion, the court somewhat surprisingly
repudiated expressly the theory of mutual subscriptions binding
each other, and also the theory of community benefit, which was
referred to as "inventing a consideration" to support a charitable
subscription. It took care, however, to pay respect to the doctrine of promissory estoppel (steps by the college in reliance on
the subscription) where properly applicable, but evidently regarded it not applicable in this case.[5]

Again the court was unanimous. It did not expressly overrule
its own decision in the Scott-Lees case, though expounding doctrines apparently at odds with it. Justices Fulton and Tilford,
respectively authors of the opinions in the two cases, participated
and concurred in both. The explanation is probably in the fact
that the Transylvania subscription did not expressly place any
specific obligation upon the university, nor name any particular
object, such as the construction of a building. Even so, a sub-

---

[4] *Hyden et al.* v. *Scott-Lees Collegiate Institute,* 291 Ky. 139, 163 S.W. 2d 295 (1942).
[5] *Floyd* v. *Transylvania University et al.,* 296 Ky. 196, 176 S.W. 2d 125, 151 A.L.R. 1230
(1943).

scription payable after death should not be confused with a will. In order to hold that the instrument in the Transylvania case was testamentary in nature, the court had to introduce considerable confusion into Kentucky law regarding subscription contracts.

Within another year the same court found itself adjudicating the case of a subscription of $5,000 to Transylvania University, payable 30 days after the death of the subscriber, with the added provision that if his wife survived him, she should receive a life annuity at six per cent of the amount. This provision was accepted in writing by the university; and Justice Thomas, speaking for the whole court, held that the university's promise to pay the annuity was a consideration sufficient to make the subscription a valid contract, enforceable against the subscriber's estate.[6]

PERFORMANCE OF THE CONDITIONS

In Pennsylvania a subscription of $5,000 was made to the Stony Brook School, in response to a drive to raise $500,000, of which $300,000 was to be allocated to erect the "John F. Carson Memorial Hall," pictured in prospectuses as a substantial and imposing three-story brick building. The subscription was conditioned: "Initial cash payment of $2,000 when construction of the John F. Carson Memorial Building is begun and balance at my convenience within five years." The drive actually realized only $95,000 cash, of which $30,000 was paid to solicitors, leaving $65,000 net. A new infirmary was constructed at a cost of about $40,000, as planned, and about $25,000 was used to renovate an ancient wooden building by reinforcing it with steel girders, installing a new foundation, and providing modern lockers and gymnasium equipment. Wooden columns were erected on the exterior face, and an inscription was placed over the door: "John Carson Auditorium and Gymnasium." The Pennsylvania supreme court correctly held that the subscription was a contract, not a gift; and that the condition had not been performed: "It is no reflection on appellee's good faith; the hard fact is that it did not perform the contract."[7] Therefore a lower court decree in favor of the school was reversed.

[6] *Transylvania University, Inc., v. Rees*, 297 Ky. 246, 179 S.W. 2d 890 (1944).
[7] *In re Carson's Estate*, 349 Pa. 529, 37 A. 2d 488 (1944).

A nondenominational junior college for girls in Denver was in severe straits in 1935, with a mortgage of $101,000 on its plant, and foreclosure threatened; $42,000 in outstanding bonds secured by second mortgage; and over $37,000 of notes and accounts unpaid. Among the unsecured debts that would have been completely wiped out had the college failed was $10,605 owed to a printing company and evidenced by a note. The first step in the college's campaign to survive was to ask the general creditors and second-mortgage bondholders (who stood to lose all in case of failure) to pledge one-half the amounts of their accounts and bonds as an incentive to other subscribers. All did so except the printing company, whose president signed a subscription of $2,500, to be credited on the $10,605 account proportionately as payments of the account were made. He also wrote "on condition that sufficient amount is secured to pay all outstanding old accounts and the second mortgage bonds."

The college continued in operation, and in 1937 broadened its subscription drive to include the building of a badly needed new dormitory. Solicitations and contributions continued until finally in 1941 payment was made in full on the last of the second-mortgage bonds and old accounts, and the college tendered the printing company the full amount of the note, less the $2,500 pledged. The company refused, demanded full payment of the note, sued, and had judgment in the trial court, which was reversed by the Colorado supreme court. The only defense against the $2,500 subscription contract was that some six years had been required for full performance of the conditions. This was obviously not a good defense, and the subscriber was bound.[8]

[8] *Colorado Woman's College* v. *Bradford-Robinson Printing Company,* 114 Colo. 237, 157 P. 2d 612 (1945).

CHAPTER XVI
THE INTERPRETATION AND EXECUTION
OF CHARITABLE BEQUESTS
TO EDUCATIONAL INSTITUTIONS

TWO types of problems are touched in the recent cases: first, constitutional and statutory limitations on the power of a testator to bequeath his estate to charitable legatees, and, secondly, the construction of testamentary provisions which appear to be vague, ambiguous, or self-contradictory.

LIMITATIONS OF TESTAMENTARY POWER

The will of a wealthy bachelor in Mississippi directed that all his lands and personal property be sold and that a large residue of his estate should go in equal parts to the University of Mississippi, Mississippi State College, and Mississippi State College for Women. His heirs-at-law, who were his second cousins, contested the will, pointing to Section 269 of the Mississippi constitution of 1890 which declares in substance that any devise of real property or any bequest of money directed to be raised by the sale of lands "to any body politic in trust, for the purpose of being appropriated to charitable uses" shall be void. The state supreme court, not without difficulty, decided that this provision must be held not to be applicable when the state is the legatee. In a dissenting opinion two of the justices contended that the constitutional limitation is on the power of the testator, and not upon the character of the devisee, and maintained that the decision of the majority opens the way for the complete destruction of its efficacy.[1]

An example of how the more common type of limitation on testamentary power may invalidate a charitable bequest in part is afforded by the case of an unmarried Iowa testatrix who bequeathed her entire estate to charitable corporations, among which was American University. She was survived by her mother, an insane person. The Iowa statute provides that no devise or bequest to charitable legatees shall be valid to the extent of more than one-fourth of the estate, if a spouse, child, child of

---

[1] *Coleman* v. *Whipple*, (Miss.), 2 So. 2d 566 (1941).

deceased child, or parent survives the testator. Hence the charitable legacies had to be scaled down to a point where their aggregate equaled no more than one-fourth of the estate. On behalf of American University it was argued that the statute was unreasonably discriminatory and therefore unconstitutional, but the court, not much impressed, remarked: "But it does not compel the testator to give his property to his relatives, nor deprive him of the right to give it all to charity during life." The litigants were reminded that the privilege of disposing of one's property by will is merely a statutory concession. The legislature has full control over descent and distribution of property, and could absolutely repeal the statute of wills if it saw fit.[2]

INTERPRETATION OF WILLS

A legendary case, entangled in litigation for more than twenty years, was that of a South Carolina testatrix who died in 1922, directing that a corporation to be known as the Trustees of the Ross Memorial be formed to care for and exhibit her collection of curios and art objects, and devising her family homestead in Charleston for the purpose. The will stipulated that all the articles must be exhibited and that no others be added to the collection.

It so happened that the museum was not opened until 1939, because several experts had testified in various earlier proceedings that only a small percentage of the articles were of museum value, and one had testified that the projected exhibit would be a "museum of bad taste." All agreed that it would add nothing to the cultural resources of Charleston. Nevertheless it was opened in 1939 and operated under a curator and appropriate assistants at a cost of about $6,400 a year, derived from funds designated in the will for that purpose.

The residuary estate amounting to some $875,000 had been bequeathed to the Presbyterian Hospital in Philadelphia and to the Medical Society of South Carolina for hospital purposes. These residuary legatees came into court alleging that the intent of the testatrix to establish a museum had failed and that the property concerned therewith should revert to the residuary estate. The court was thus faced with a choice between two

[2] *Decker* v. *American University et al.*, (Iowa), 20 N.W. 2d 466 (1945).

charitable purposes. It readily reached the conclusion that the museum trust was invalid because it conferred no public benefits. "The object and effect of every charitable bequest is to confer a public benefit, else it would be no charity," said the state supreme court in affirming the decision.[3]

No sooner was the museum trust disposed of than it was discovered that the codicil of 1921 which created it had revoked an earlier devise of the homestead property to the Charleston Library Society; and the court was faced with the difficult question of whether the codicil had absolutely and finally revoked the devise to the Library, or whether it must be regarded under the circumstances as merely a conditional revocation, so that the devise to the Library would be revived by the invalidation of the museum trust. The issue being between the Medical Society and the Library, the court looked at the will as a whole and considered the two types of purposes, and concluded that it was the testatrix's chief intent to give the homestead and other property (about one-fourth of her estate) to "cultural and educational purposes," and the rest of her estate to hospital purposes. Accordingly it decreed that the Library should take the property of the defunct museum trust.[4]

Thereupon the Medical Society and its companion legatee, the Presbyterian Hospital in Philadelphia, sued to recover their outlay of $1,360 expended in the suit to invalidate the museum trust. They alleged that their loss of that sum was caused by *laches* on the part of the Library Society in neglecting to assert its claim in court until nineteen years after the will was probated. The court somewhat testily declared that there was no issue of *laches* under the circumstances of this case; but nevertheless, as an exercise of its equity jurisdiction, awarded the plaintiffs $1,360 out of funds going to the Library, "solely to make them whole by reimbursing them" for outlays actually made.[5]

Perhaps emboldened by this result, attorneys who had represented the Medical Society on a contingent fee basis next sued to

---

[3] *Medical Society of South Carolina et al.* v. *South Carolina National Bank of Charleston*, 197 S.C. 96, 14 S.E. 2d 577 (1941).
[4] *Charleston Library Society et al.* v. *Citizens' and Southern National Bank et al.*, 200 S.C. 96, 20 S.E. 2d 623 (1942).
[5] *Charleston Library Society et al.* v. *Citizens' and Southern National Bank et al.*, 201 S.C. 477, 23 S.E. 2d 362 (1942).

recover their fees from the Library Society, but without success. Looking at the position of the Library Society and its co-suitors as successful litigants, the court admonished that "It would be a hard measure of justice if they were also required to pay the counsel of their adversaries."[6]

Executors of Will Cannot Go Beyond Intent Expressed in the Instrument

A wealthy testatrix in Connecticut died in 1939, bequeathing a large residuary estate to such charitable, benevolent, religious, or educational institutions as the executors should select. One of the executors possessed a list of institutions in which the testatrix was interested, including the "Fund for Near East Colleges," which she had given him. The executors petitioned for permission to organize a nonprofit corporation to receive the funds of the estate and make distribution over a period of years. The court decided that the proposed scheme was too great a deviation from the testatrix's expressed intent.[7]

The aspects of this case concerned with the Connecticut succession tax have already been noticed in Chapter XII.

Inconsistent Provisions Will Not Be Stricken Down If Reconcilable in Light of Testator's General Intention

A St. Louis testator gave $10,000 to Washington University, but the language of the will was such as to make it impossible to determine with certainty whether he intended this gift to be unconditional, or whether he intended it to lapse if a sale of certain shares of stock in his estate did not occur by a specified date. The ambiguity arose from the wording of two separate and mutually inconsistent paragraphs. The supreme court of Missouri, in holding that the gift was meant to be unconditional, said:

> It seems to us that the whole will discloses the intention of the testator to make provision for his family *and* for unconditional gifts to Church and University, and we hold that the bequests to Church and University will not lapse and be determined if the shares of stock are, or are not, sold by November 25, 1947. . . .

6 *Bedford et al.* v. *Citizens' and Southern National Bank et al.*, 203 S.C. 507, 28 S.E. 2d 405 (1943).
7 *Cochran et al.* v. *McLaughlin et al.*, 128 Conn. 638, 24 A. 2d 836 (1942).

These conclusions give effect to both of the apparently conflicting provisions of the will in harmony with the real intent of the testator, as we believe it to have been, as disclosed by the language of the whole will.

The last sentence is a statement of one of the cardinal rules for the interpretation of ambiguous or self-contradictory wills.[8]

TESTAMENTARY DESIGNATION OF AN EDUCATIONAL PURPOSE

A will bequeathing $1,000,000 in trust "for the purpose of founding, erecting and maintaining a museum of art to be known as 'Everson Museum of Art' to be located in the city of Syracuse, New York" was contested by heirs of the testatrix who alleged that there was nothing in the terms of the will to interdict operation of the trust for private profit, and that the purpose was not educational because there was no specific provision for instruction or reading materials and because the testatrix had been heard to express during her life a distaste for the use of the existing Syracuse Museum of Art as a place of instruction for small children. Neither of these contentions was sustained, and it was held that the will created a valid charitable trust. On the issue of educational purpose, the court's quotation from the old New Hampshire case of *Sargent* v. *Cornish* (54 N.H. 18) is of especial interest:[9]

> Educational purposes are 'not merely the means of instruction in grammar or mathematics, or the arts and sciences, but all that series of instruction and discipline which is intended to enlighten the understanding, correct the temper, purify the heart, elevate the affections, and to inculcate generous and patriotic sentiments, and to form the manners and habits of rising generations, and so fit them for usefulness in their future stations. And the means of education are not solely books and printed rules and maxims, but representations and symbols and pageantry, it may be.'

---

[8] *Lang et al.* v. *Taussig et al.*, (Mo.), 180 S.W. 2d 698 (1944).

[9] *In re Everson's Will*, 268 App. Div. 425, 52 N.Y.S. 2d 395 (1944); motion for leave to appeal denied, and motion for new trial denied, 269 App. Div. 727, 54 N.Y.S. 2d 696 (1945); appeal granted, 294 N.Y. 640, 62 N.E. 2d 247 (1945); affirmed, 295 N.Y. 622, 64 N.E. 2d 653 (1945).

CHAPTER XVII
THE CREATION AND OPERATION OF
CHARITABLE TRUSTS FOR HIGHER EDUCATION

NEW sets of facts constantly arise to require new decisions regarding the creation and validity of charitable trusts, the distinctions between charitable and private trusts, the character of "living trusts" over which the donor retains control, the meeting of conditions by the trustee, the application of the judicial doctrine of *cy pres*, and the disposition of trusts which are alleged to have failed.

DESIGNATION OF BENEFICIARIES

The will of an Alabama resident directed his executor to sell, lease, or otherwise dispose of specified property and turn the net proceeds over to some institution for the purpose of research as to the cause and cure of arthritis. The executor chose the medical school of the University of Alabama, and a trial court decree approving the disposition was affirmed by the supreme court of Alabama, though the validity of the trust was attacked on the ground that no definite beneficiary was designated in the will. Said the court: "The trust created by the will is not a trust in which the ultimate beneficiaries are to be selected. It is a trust for the purpose of research, educational in its scope and purpose, for the benefit of a class designated by the testator in the will."[1]

CAPACITY OF TRUSTEE TO TAKE

The leaseholders of real property in Baltimore questioned and resisted the transfer of title to the property under the will of the owner, a wealthy Jewish testatrix, who devised the ground rents "one-half to the Associated Jewish Charities of Baltimore and the other half thereof to the Hebrew University of Jerusalem; to be applied to the respective purposes of said corporations." It was shown that the correct nomenclature of the latter devisee was "Hebrew University Association," and it was alleged to be an unincorporated association and as such incapable of holding or conveying real property in Maryland. The testimony of an expert on Palestinian law, however, demonstrated that the

[1] *Hinson v. Smyer*, (Ala.), 21 So. 2d 825 (1945).

Hebrew University Association, formed in 1925 and operating under the "Law of Societies" dating from 1909 under the Ottoman regime, which law was retained in force under the British mandate following World War I, had all the necessary powers to receive the devise, and to convert it into funds of the Association. The court concluded that the Association was "clothed with all the attributes of a body corporate, and functions as such." It was therefore held that the devise created a charitable trust, and the devisee was a charitable corporation within the meaning of the Maryland statute of 1931 which recognized the principles of the Statute of 43 Elizabeth (1602) and abrogated the common-law rule under which an unincorporated devisee could not receive a testamentary gift. To the plaintiffs' contention that the Palestinian Law of Societies requires such associations to obtain specific authorization from the Government of Palestine in transactions of this type, the court answered that any limitation imposed by foreign law on the right of an association organized thereunder to hold and dispose of realty has no extraterritorial force.[2]

DISTINCTION BETWEEN PRIVATE AND CHARITABLE TRUSTS

The will of a New York testator recited: "The balance of said one-half trust fund after making the aforesaid two payments shall be paid and disposed of by my said executors and trustees to any charitable institution or institutions or to any person, persons, individual or individuals that my said executors and trustees seek [*sic*] fit and proper." This clause created no charitable trust, "since authority to distribute to any person or individual subjects the whole fund to a distribution for private purposes."[3]

The Topeka Chapter of the Daughters of the American Revolution of Kansas, having given Washburn College a $1,250 fund in the early 1920's to provide one annual scholarship for a war veteran to be selected by the college, sought to recover the fund because no student beneficiary was selected in 1944, a year for which the income accumulated and unused was $40.31. The gift had been made with neither limitation as to time nor provi-

---

[2] *Reisig et al. v. Associated Jewish Charities of Baltimore et al.*, 182 Md. 432, 34 A. 2d 842 (1943).

[3] *In re Sheifer's Estate*, 178 Misc. 340, 34 N.Y.S. 2d 302 (1942).

sion for reversion, and the fact that Washburn College in 1941 transferred its plant to Washburn Municipal University of Topeka was adjudged not to affect the issue. One of the arguments for the Chapter was that the gift created a private trust, not charitable. After quoting, "There cannot be a private trust unless there is a beneficiary who is definitely ascertained at the time of the creation of the trust or definitely ascertainable within the period of the rule against perpetuities," the court concluded:

> We think it may not be said a private trust was created. The income of the trust was not to be devoted to the use of definitely ascertained persons, but to a person to be selected from a class. Neither can it be said it was not beneficial to the community because the net income was sufficient to pay tuition of only one student. Such a test solely applied would make a large fund charitable and a small fund private, and certainly that is not a true test.

Accordingly a judgment perpetuating the trust was affirmed.[4]

THE REVOCABLE "LIVING TRUST" WITH COLLEGE AS REMAINDERMAN

Typical of the universal human yearning to "have one's cake and eat it too" is the desire of men of means to establish while living trusts for the benefit of their surviving dependents, and ultimately for charitable purposes, coupled with reluctance to part with the income or the control of the funds while they live. Thus we have "living trusts" which the donor reserves the right to revoke, and in which he stipulates that all or a portion of the income shall accrue to him during his lifetime. Such a trust serves the purpose of providing for his private beneficiaries and affords an expeditious method of handling the property at his death. Sometimes he also retains some measure of control over the management of the trust for the duration of his life. There must be a line beyond which he cannot go in these directions without vitiating the trust and making it a mere personal agency which will expire at his death.[5] The point is of great import to colleges and universities, for such institutions are often the ulti-

---

[4] *Daughters of the American Revolution of Kansas, Topeka Chapter*, v. *Washburn College*, 160 Kan. 583, 164 P. 2d 128 (1945).

[5] Several Ohio cases bearing on this question are analyzed by Robert P. Goldman and Evans L. De Camp in "When Is a Trust Not a Trust?" *University of Cincinnati Law Review*, Vol. 16, pp. 191–218 (May 1942).

mate remaindermen designated to receive the trust after the death of the surviving specified private beneficiaries.

An example is afforded by an Ohio case in which the donor had named the Central Trust Company of Cincinnati as trustee of certain securities, but reserved to himself the right to direct their investment and reinvestment, and the right to revoke the trust. He also retained the right to the income as long as he lived. The trust instrument specified that from the day of his death an annuity should be paid to his daughter for the duration of her life, and the balance of the net income should go to his wife during her lifetime. The remainder was to go to such institution or individual as the donor during his lifetime might in writing designate; or, failing that, as his widow might similarly designate; or, failing that, to Dartmouth College. The donor never revoked the trust, and never exercised the power to appoint the remainderman. His widow exercised the power of appointment by naming Dartmouth College, with certain conditions and reservations. Later she tried to change the appointment by naming Berea College. After her death, and with the daughter still living, the trustee had accumulated sufficient income to make a preliminary transfer to whichever college was entitled to it, and sued for instructions from the court. The issue between the two colleges was decided in favor of Berea in the trial court and in the intermediate appellate court, holding that the power of appointment reserved to the widow was valid, and was not exhausted by its first exercise.

When the case reached the Ohio supreme court, that tribunal, of its own motion, ordered a reargument on the question of the validity of the entire trust. The trustee and both colleges thereupon filed briefs and argued for the validity of the trust, which was sustained by the narrowly divided vote of four justices against three. One of the four took pains to explain in a specially concurring opinion that his view was merely that the trust could not be attacked after it had been acquiesced in for thirty years by all persons entitled to beneficial interests in the donor's estate. The same four judges joined in holding that the widow's power of appointment was valid, but was exhausted by its first exercise. Thus Dartmouth was the remainderman.[6]

The strength of the dissent may presage a revolt from some

---

[6] *Central Trust Company of Cincinnati* v. *Watt*, 139 Ohio St. 50, 38 N.E. 2d 185 (1941).

former doctrines. The three dissenting justices said the trust was invalid because (1) while the donor lived and possessed his reserved power to revoke it, no one could acquire a vested interest in the remainder; and (2) the donor reserved such powers of control as to create merely an agency, which was revoked by his death.

The preponderance of judicial opinion in Ohio and elsewhere is that a "living trust" is not invalid solely because it is revocable during the donor's life, and public policy would seem to support that view. It should be observed, however, that unsatisfied creditors of the donor can reach, at least during his lifetime, the principal of a revocable trust from which he receives the income. In other words, a trust must become irrevocable before it acquires immunity from the creditors of its founder.

When the Gift Is Conditional, the Trustee Must Qualify by Meeting the Stipulated Conditions

In Ohio a residuary estate of a quarter of a million dollars was bequeathed in trust in 1938 for the founding of a Protestant industrial school. The fund was to be offered first to the city of Conneaut, on condition that the municipality provide a good site and issue 5 per cent bonds in the amount of $100,000, or otherwise provide a capital that would produce $5,000 a year income for the school. If Conneaut did not qualify, the alternative offeree was to be the village of Geneva, on the same terms; and if Geneva did not qualify, then the trustee bank was directed either to set up a corporation to found the school, or to give the trust fund to some existing industrial school. Conneaut did not accept. Geneva accepted by resolution and ordinance, but encountered obstacles in meeting the condition, because the projected school is held to be sectarian, and the Ohio constitution prohibits the use of tax funds for sectarian institutions.

When asked for a declaratory judgment to instruct the trustee, the Ohio supreme court decided in 1945 that Geneva must be given a further reasonable time in which to qualify, and defined "reasonable time" as one year from the date of the judgment. Although the trust fund had increased to $900,000 since 1938, the court declined to authorize a deviation from the terms of the trust whereby the increment could be regarded as the source of the stipulated $5,000 annual income, in lieu of the condition imposed on the municipality.[7]

Execution of Charitable Trust Where Donor's Intent Was to Authorize Discretionary Latitude

During the years 1926–28 the General Education Board, a Rockefeller philanthropic foundation, gave the Trustees of Teachers College, a corporation affiliated with Columbia University, an aggregate of $3,000,000 as endowment, "the income to be used for the support of the Lincoln School of Teachers College in order to insure the permanence of experimental work in the field of elementary and secondary education." When in 1940 the trustees determined to merge the Lincoln School with the Horace Mann School, a demonstration school also operated by Teachers College, an injunction to prevent the merger on the ground that it would be an unlawful departure from the purpose of the gifts was sought by certain pupils of the Lincoln School, parents, an unincorporated association of teachers and parents, and an individual who had contributed to a building fund for the school.

The injunction was denied and the merger adjudged permissible. The Lincoln School was merely an unincorporated agency of Teachers College, and the deciding factor was in the general policies of the General Education Board regarding all its gifts, to the effect that they "shall always be regarded as available for use in the broadest way so as best to promote the purpose"; and that, after the lapse of ten years following the gift, it was desired to permit the donee to have free discretion as to whether the general purpose could be better served by using the gift for some specific purpose other than that for which it was originally made, "such specific purpose to be as closely akin to the original purpose as may be found practicable at the time."[8]

---

[7] *Findley et al.* v. *City of Conneaut et al.*, 145 Ohio St. 480, 62 N.E. 2d 318 (1945), modifying *Same*, 76 Ohio App. 153, 63 N.E. 2d 449 (1945).

[8] *Elliott et al.* v. *Teachers College et al.*, 177 Misc. 746, 31 N.Y.S. 2d 796 (1941); affirmed without opinion, 264 App. Div. 839, 35 N.Y.S. 761 (1942); motion for leave to appeal denied, 264 App. Div. 917, 36 N.Y.S. 2d 238 (1942); appeal granted, 43 N.E. 2d 357 (1942); affirmed, 290 N.Y. 747, 50 N.E. 2d 97 (1943).

The Judicial Doctrine of Cy Pres:
"Equity May Mold the Trust"

The doctrine under which courts of equity authorize modifications of the terms of charitable trust instruments when necessary to preserve and perpetuate the trust to effectuate the charitable intent of the donor in the face of changing conditions unforeseen by him, and especially changes occurring long after his death, has been embodied in clear form in a statute of the state of New York:

> ... whenever it is shown to the court that the circumstances have so changed since the execution of an instrument containing a charitable gift, ... as to render impracticable or impossible a literal compliance with the terms of such instrument, the court may, upon application of the trustee ... make an order directing that such gift shall be administered or expended in such manner as in the judgment of the court will most effectually accomplish the general purpose of the testator, without regard to and free from any specific restriction, limitation or direction contained in the instrument.

The principle was applied in the case of a testratrix who died in 1891, bequeathing all her books, manuscripts, paintings and other works of art to the trustees of the Lenox Library in New York, on condition of acceptance within ninety days, and stipulating that the gift be designated "The Robert L. Stuart Collection" and be housed in a separate room of the library building, open to the public at reasonable times, but "never to be exhibited on the Lord's Day." The library accepted and complied with the conditions. Later it was consolidated with the Astor and Tilden libraries to form the "New York Public Library, Astor, Lenox and Tilden Foundations." Fifty years after the death of the testratrix this corporation applied for court approval of projected deviations from the original stipulations, on account of changed conditions and pressure for space in the Public Library building. Specifically, it sought permission to mingle the books with the general library and lend the rest of the collection to the New York Historical Society, which had good housing facilities and was willing to accept the loan if freed from the requirement of separate room, separate catalogue, and Sunday closing. The collection appeared to be in part a sociological and historical record of New York City in the nineteenth century, of some historic interest but of no great artistic merit or pecuniary value.

The court concluded that "The passage of time since . . . 1891 and the changed and liberalized conditions throughout this long period of over fifty years, justify . . . the relaxing of the restrictions imposed as to the preservation, maintenance and exhibition of the Collection and particularly the prohibition of its exhibition on Sunday." The American Bible Society, as one of thirty-three residuary legatees, contended that relaxation of the Sunday rule caused a failure of the trust, thus letting the property fall into the residuary estate. This contention the court did not sustain.[9]

A wealthy resident of the District of Columbia executed a will in 1936 providing for the erection of a memorial building to house his manuscripts and art objects, naming three educational institutions in the South as alternative sites, in order of his preference: Duke University, the University of North Carolina, and Rollins College. Subsequently the president of Duke University gave him oral assurances that Duke University would accept the trust. Accordingly in 1938 he made a new will designating that institution alone for the purpose. He died in 1940, and in 1941 the executive committee of the governing board of Duke University declined to accept the trust. Thereupon his next of kin sued to recover the trust fund, on the ground that the trust had failed. Judgment was for the plaintiffs in the District Court, but was reversed and remanded by the Court of Appeals, sustaining the validity of the trust and holding it a proper case for the application of the doctrine of *cy pres* to give effect to the donor's charitable intent: "The dominant idea in the mind of the testator was the cause of art in the South." The Supreme Court of the United States declined to review the case, and accordingly the District Court subsequently dismissed the suit of the next of kin and realigned the other parties for a determination of the remaining issues, and this judgment was affirmed by the Court of Appeals. Another feature of the will, setting up a separate trust to provide for certain annual prizes at Rollins College, was also sustained.[10]

---

[9] *In re Stuart's Estate*, (N.Y. Surrogate), 183 Misc. 20, 46 N.Y.S. 2d 911 (1944).

[10] *Noel et al.* v. *Olds et al.*, (U.S.C.A. for D.C.), 138 F. 2d 581 (1943); certiorari denied, 321 U.S. 773, 64 S. Ct. 611, 88 L. Ed. 1067 (1944); and *Same*, (U.S.C.A. for D.C.), 149 F. 2d 13 (1945).

PERPETUATION OF EDUCATIONAL TRUSTS AS AGAINST
ALLEGATIONS OF FAILURE

The period affords three examples of attempts, all unsuccessful, to have educational trusts adjudged to have failed or terminated. The Funk Seminary at La Grange, Kentucky, was established in 1841 by a bequest of $10,000 on condition that the citizens of Oldham County would raise $500 additional. It was operated continuously until 1911, when its building was destroyed by fire. At that time a suit against its trustees by the county superintendent of schools was pending, in which he alleged that the old building was inadequate and unsafe for school purposes and asked that it be sold and the proceeds combined with funds of the county board of education and of the La Grange graded school district to erect a new public school building. He obtained a favorable judgment, the property was sold for $5,220, and that sum was applied to a new public school building bearing the words "Funk Seminary" across its front. On its diplomas and letterheads the name of the school was printed as "Funk Seminary and Oldham County High School."

In 1938 the descendants of certain heirs and residuary devisees of the original donor came into court asking that the trust be declared abandoned and terminated, so that the original gift would revert to them. Their suit failed, because the highest court of the state held that the trust must continue as long as it is possible to approximate the charitable intent of the donor; and it may operate in conjunction with the public school authorities if that appears to be the best way to effectuate his intent. In fact, this procedure actually saved the trust from failure, thought the court, rather than causing it to fail. It was immaterial that the complainants were not made parties to the suit of 1911, because they could not then have asserted any more rights than they assert today.[11]

The rule that "no trust shall be permitted to fail for want of a trustee" is exemplified in the case of a resident of the town of Mt. Vernon in Kennebec County, Maine, who devised his house and lot in trust to the town for use as a public library. He also bequeathed his residuary estate in trust to the executor of

---

[11] *Harwood v. Dick*, 286 Ky. 423, 150 S.W. 2d 704 (1941).

his will, the income thereof to be used to keep the house in repair and purchase suitable books. In two or three successive town meetings there was much controversy and confusion regarding the matter, with the result that the town did not accept the real property in trust, though there is some doubt that there was any clear-cut refusal of it. There was some evidence that the sole heir-at-law of the donor attempted to influence the town to reject the gift. This heir laid claim to the whole estate on the ground that the trust had failed, whereupon the executor sued for a construction of the will. The decree was that the trust must be sustained and, if necessary, the court in the exercise of its equity jurisdiction would name a trustee. Eventually the court designated three persons as trustees in place of the town. These persons, after having remodeled the house for library purposes and ascertained that the principal of the residuary estate in trust was $29,000, to be increased by $10,000 upon the termination of certain life estates, came into court asking permission to use a part of the income for operating expenses. Their petition was denied because the will made no provision for operating expenses, and there was no proof that they could not be provided from some other source; but when again the trustees came with such evidence, the court authorized the use of part of the income for operating expenses, as an exercise of the *cy pres* power to prevent the failure of the trust.[12]

A less clear case is one wherein a Missouri donor gave $2,000 to an individual as special trustee and directed that the income be used to keep in repair Litchfield Hall, a dormitory on the campus of Martha Washington College at Abingdon, Virginia. The transaction took place in 1919, and in the same year the trustees of the college conveyed all its property to Emory and Henry College, a coeducational institution located nine miles away and operated under the same denominational auspices (Methodist Episcopal Church, South); but the deed remained unrecorded until 1929, and Martha Washington College was operated as a separate institution until 1931, when its doors were closed. Thereafter its plant was leased for a long term to a hotel company, and is now used as a commercially operated hotel. The special trustee of the $2,000 laid claim to the fund in her own

---

[12] *Manufacturers National Bank* v. *Woodward*, 138 Me. 70, 21 A. 2d 705 (1941); *Same*, 140 Me. 117, 34 A. 2d 471 (1943); and *Same*, 141 Me. 28, 38 A. 2d 657 (1944).

right, because the original donor, a lady at the age of 90, upon being told that the college no longer existed, had expressed a desire that the trustee should have the fund.

The highest court of Virginia decided against the claim by a vote of four of the judges against three. The majority, proceeding upon the theory that a valid and effective voluntary trust is irrevocable, concluded that this trust ought to continue because there is still a Litchfield Hall for the benefit of which the donor created the trust, chiefly to perpetuate the family name. Although the hall is not at present used as a dormitory for women on the campus of an educational institution, yet it is still owned by the church body which sponsored the defunct college, and it is easily conceivable that it might again be used for educational purposes.[13] Justice Holt, speaking for the minority of the court, acridly criticized this view. As to the use of the hall at the time of the suit, he said:

> Now in the lessees' advertisement, it is designated as 'N. W. Inn New Ball Room.' In it is held the annual tobacco ball, with a floor show and other dancers. It is used for commercial purposes; in it a Democratic Convention has been held; a state liquor dealers' convention might be. A more complete perversion of the purposes for which it was intended is hard to picture. The purpose of the trust has definitely failed.

Failure of Trust Where Charitable Intent Was Specific and Not General

In 1905 a decedent in Waterbury, Connecticut, bequeathed an estate of approximately $30,000, part realty and part personalty, to trustees to establish a school or college to be operated in accord with a plan specified in considerable detail, including six-month winter terms for young men to be alternated with summer periods of remunerative work, and three-month summer terms for young women, thus avoiding coeducation. The donor was known to be somewhat eccentric and vigorously opposed to customary educational methods, wishing to found an institution that would revolutionize them, and expecting that gifts from other donors would augment the fund. No other gifts were received, and on account of the insufficiency of the fund, no school was established. By 1944 the value of the corpus had grown to $196,-

---

[13] *Penn v. Keller et al.,* 178 Va. 131, 16 S.E. 2d 331 (1941).

000 through advantageous sales of property and stocks. At this stage the disposition of the trust was litigated, the question being whether the fund could properly be turned over to the town of Waterbury to be used in the establishment of a state trade school, or whether it should go to the heirs of the original donor. The decision was that the fund could not go to the town for state trade-school purposes, because the donor's motive was clearly not a general benevolent intent to aid any kind of school indiscriminately, and state trade schools do not operate on a plan such as he prescribed. The "doctrine of approximation" is not applicable where the charitable intent is specifically defined and not general, thought the court. Moreover, the fact that the fund had not become large enough for the purpose after forty years, and the very dim prospects of its future rapid growth, were thought to justify the finding that the trust had failed definitely, and that the heirs-at-law should be allowed to assert their interest, though this must be done in a subsequent separate action because the pleadings in the present case were not inclusive of that purpose.[14]

---

[14] *Waterbury Trust Company* v. *Porter et al.*, 131 Conn. 206, 38 A. 2d 598 (1944).

CHAPTER XVIII
THE TORT RESPONSIBILITY
OF STATE AND MUNICIPAL INSTITUTIONS

STEMMING from the ancient doctrine that "the King can do no wrong," and rationalized in various ways, the immunity of the state and its agencies from responsibility for injuries to private persons continues to be generally maintained, as is evidenced by recent decisions in Wisconsin, Michigan, Missouri, and Texas. Under this theory the only recourse against the state open to the innocent aggrieved party is an approach to the legislature for a special act granting indemnity outright or authorizing the case to be adjudicated. New York exhibits a tendency to temper the harshness of the common law, both by judicial decision and by general statute, including a Court of Claims Act. In some states the employees of state institutions are protected by workmen's compensation laws, but no state has a scheme of social insurance covering injuries to innocent parties under all circumstances.

WISCONSIN

A young man, standing up on his seat at a football game in the Camp Randall Stadium at the University of Wisconsin in 1938, was pushed over the edge of an exit by pressure of the crowd and fell twelve feet, receiving serious injuries. He proceeded against the state and the regents of the university under the so-called "safe place" statute, which requires the state and all municipal or other subdivisions to take care that places where the public is invited to congregate shall be kept in a safe condition. This statute, said the state supreme court, merely defines a standard of care, the absence of which constitutes negligence, and it does not go so far as to create a right of action against the state. The court then relied upon the familiar rule of immunity: "No cause of action exists against the state on account of the wrongful acts of its officers or agents unless the state has clearly and definitely consented that it shall be so liable."[1]

---

[1] *Holzworth* v. *State*, 238 Wis. 63, 298 N.W. 163 (1941).

MICHIGAN: MUNICIPAL UNIVERSITY AS STATE AGENCY

At Wayne University in Detroit a sophomore in the college of medicine lost his life in 1937 by falling down an elevator shaft in the medical school building. His father, suing for indemnity, alleged negligence in the maintenance and inspection of the automatic elevator; and indeed the evidence showed that, when the elevator was not at the floor, the door could be opened on account of a defective latch mechanism. On his behalf it was also argued that the practice of the college of medicine in restricting admissions and charging substantial tuition fees made it partake of the nature of a proprietary enterprise, and thus precluded its defense of immunity as a strictly public governmental activity. This contention was brushed aside upon the showing that the tuition fees were less than thirty per cent of the cost of operation; and judgment for the defendant on the ground of non-liability as a state agency was affirmed. "We conclude," said the supreme court of Michigan, "that the defendant, in owning and operating Wayne University college of medicine, was a State agency exercising a purely governmental function and was not liable for the alleged negligence of its agents and employees."[2]

TEXAS

A laborer employed by the Texas Agricultural and Mechanical College at one of its experiment stations was given a spray-pump and instructed to spray a building. He claimed that by reason of a defect in the pump, liquid was squirted into his eye, causing loss of the eye. The trial court sustained a general exception to his petition, but the Court of Civil Appeals thought the case should go back for trial, declaring with vigor: "The proposition that the State owes to an employee the nondelegable duties of an employer is sustained by justice, logic, and authoritative precedent"; and, "The right of control and direction should not be conferred without some legal obligation in respect thereto." The next higher court, however, elected to stand on the well-worn doctrine of the immunity of the state while engaged in the performance of its governmental functions. Accord-

[2] *Daszkiewicz* v. *Board of Education of City of Detroit*, 301 Mich. 212, 3 N.W. 2d 71 (1942).

ingly it reversed the decision of the Court of Civil Appeals and affirmed the judgment of the trial court, thus leaving the injured man with no remedy as against the state.[3]

Another demonstration of state immunity was made by a Texas court when a claimant seeking to get possession of two tracts of land held by the University of Texas, and damages for four months' rental aggregating $600, brought a statutory action of trespass to try title. Dismissal of the suit was affirmed by the Court of Civil Appeals, using the following words and reasoning: "The University and the Board of Regents are institutions of the State, and neither has any existence independent of the State. .... Property belonging to the University of Texas is the property of the State." Therefore the state would be a necessary party to the suit, and the court was without jurisdiction to hear it unless the pleadings contained an allegation and showing of consent by the state to be sued.[4]

KENTUCKY

At eleven o'clock on an autumn evening an automobile dashed through the campus of a state teachers college in western Kentucky, exceeding the local speed limit. The uniformed night watchman shouted to halt the car, without result. He fired his pistol, aiming at a rear tire of the receding vehicle. The bullet struck the pavement and ricocheted into the car, killing one of the occupants. The watchman had been employed by the college for some seventeen years. In order to clothe him with power to make arrests, he had been made nominally a member of the local city police force, subject to the orders of the mayor. Actually he had never received any orders from the mayor, nor any pay from the city, and was in fact a full-time employee of the college. Damages for the death of his victim were sought in a suit in which five defendants were joined in order to cover all possibilities: the watchman, the surety company on his bond as an employee of the college, the college itself, the city, and the state as owner of the college. The suit was instituted after the Kentucky legislature had passed a special resolution authorizing it to be brought against

---

[3] *State* v. *Morgan*, 140 Tex. 620, 170 S.W. 2d 652 (1943), reversing (Tex. Civ. App.), 170 S.W. 2d 648 (1943).
[4] *Walsh* v. *University of Texas*, (Tex. Civ. App.), 169 S.W. 2d 993 (1943).

the state and the college, and stipulating that the damages, if awarded, were to be paid out of the general fund of the state and not out of funds appropriated to the college.

The trial court incorrectly found that the watchman was acting as a police officer of the city at the time of the shooting, and not as an agent of the college. Accordingly, the state and the college would not be liable, and the city would be immune under the rule that municipal corporations are not responsible for torts of their employees engaged in strictly governmental functions. The surety company could not be held because its bond obviously was not drawn to cover the case. A judgment for $800 was entered against the watchman personally. The Kentucky Court of Appeals, upon reviewing the case, remanded it for a new trial on several grounds. Approving that part of the decision which exonerated the city and the surety company, the court pointed out that the conclusion regarding the relation of the state and the college to the watchman was obviously erroneous. Moreover, an award of $800 for death is manifestly meager, and its apparent insufficiency would justify a new trial on that score, thought the court. Another error in the proceedings at the trial was the admission of testimony that shooting at tires to stop speeding automobiles is common practice among peace officers. In fact, that practice had already been held to constitute criminal negligence in Kentucky; and the watchman defendant in this case had already been indicted for involuntary manslaughter in separate criminal proceedings.

It was argued by the defense that the special resolution of the legislature authorizing the liability of the state to be adjudicated in this case should be held invalid, because it allegedly conflicted with the section of the Kentucky Constitution prohibiting the enactment of local or special legislation. The majority of the court was unimpressed, but on this point alone three of the judges dissented, believing that the state's permission to be sued if given at all, must be given by a general legislative act. Thus, after a somewhat tortuous sequence of events, the ultimate result of the actions of the legislature and the court of last resort in this case made it one in which the way was opened for the aggrieved party to obtain adequate indemnity from the state. This came about, however, only because the case was such that the legislature could be prevailed upon to grant a special dispensation; and even the legislature's power to do that was seriously questioned.[5]

NEW YORK

A more advanced trend, already noted in earlier years in New York, continued. A girl student at the Oneonta State Normal School attended a musical rehearsal in the auditorium on the second floor of a campus building at four o'clock on a December afternoon in 1937. At a little after five o'clock she left the room, groped through the unlighted hall to the stairway, and fell down the stairway because the handrail for which she was groping did not reach all the way up to the landing but was two or three steps short. The state court of claims denied her any indemnification, but the appellate division, third department, reversed the decision and awarded her a judgment for $13,218 damages. The gist of the opinion, in which all five judges concurred, may be gathered from the words of Judge Schenck:[6]

> I think that on this evidence, the state is liable. Having permitted, if indeed it did not invite, claimant to be in the auditorium at 5 o'clock and thereafter, it should have provided a safe exit. Claimant was carrying books, as, of course, any student customarily would while engaged in curricular or extracurricular activities. It was natural for her to carry the books in her right arm, and this would reasonably lead her to descend the left hand side of the stairs in order to use the handrail on that side. It being dark, and especially as both floor and handrail were black, she was obliged to grope and feel her way. The fact that the rail did not go all the way to the landing might have been all right under proper lighting conditions, but under these circumstances the lack of a handrail for several steps, taken in connection with a total lack of light, seems to me to constitute negligence.

New York afforded another example of the more humane theory. A Syracuse city policeman was injured on property of the New York State College of Forestry adjacent to Syracuse University, while performing his duties in keeping order and preventing rowdyism at a night football game. He was part of a detail of thirty policemen sent to the premises at the request of the university. While posting his men at strategic points outside the stadium at about seven o'clock P.M., before the floodlights had

5 *Daniels' Administrator* v. *Hoofnel et al.*, 287 Ky. 834, 155 S.W. 2d 469 (1941).

6 *Hovey* v. *State*, 261 App. Div. 759, 262 App. Div. 791, 27 N.Y.S. 2d 195 (1941); affirmed, 287 N.Y. 663, 39 N.E. 2d 287 (1941).

been turned on, he proceeded on foot at a moderate pace on a macadam roadway alongside the stadium. Unknown to him, a heavy chain had been stretched across the road, and in the darkness he fell over it and was injured. There was no light or other warning signal at or near the chain. The road was on the campus of the State College of Forestry, and the key to the chain was in possession of the Dean or other employee of the college.

On first hearing of the injured man's claim, the case was dismissed for lack of technical compliance with provisions of the Court of Claims Act; but the legislature enacted a statute in 1943 authorizing the court to hear and determine the case notwithstanding. When the case eventually came for decision on the merits, an award of damages was made. Said the Court of Claims: "The State as well as the university owed to the claimant, in the performance of his requested duties, the exercise of reasonable care in the maintenance of its premises."[7]

In a clearer case a 19-year-old boy who was a student at the New York State Agricultural and Technical Institute at Delhi was awarded indemnity for injuries sustained by falling from a 20-foot scaffold while working as a student carpenter under the supervision of instructors. The Court of Claims found: "The testimony is convincing that it was the failure of the state to comply with the statutory requirement of a proper railing that was the proximate cause of the accident"; and pointed out: "The state, under Section 8 of the Court of Claims Act, has waived its immunity from liability for the negligence of its agents in its charitable and other institutions."[8]

INDIANA

In Indiana the New Harmony Memorial Commission was created by a statute of 1939 to purchase and restore sites and buildings and administer a variety of other activities designed to commemorate appropriately the famous nineteenth-century experiment in communal living at the village of New Harmony. It was given power "to institute programs and projects of an educational, recreational, patriotic and cultural nature . . . such as forums, lyceums, balls, festivals, and public astronomical ob-

---

[7] *Leahy* v. *State*, (N.Y. Ct. Claims), 46 N.Y.S. 2d 310 (1944).

[8] *Weber* v. *State*, 181 Misc. 44, 43 N.Y.S. 2d 645 (1943), 267 App. Div. 325, 45 N.Y.S. 2d 834 (1944), 53 N.Y.S. 2d 598 (1945).

servations; ... geological expeditions ...; scientific, literary, historical, and philosophical institutes in memory of Robert Owen and his illustrious sons, and other eminent leaders of Owenite days. ..." The statute also specified that "arrangements may be made with one or more higher institutions of learning in Indiana or with individual members of faculties thereof for the most economical and effective promotion of the uses and purposes of this act; and the most favorable working relations shall be cultivated at all times with public and parochial schools of Indiana. ..."

The commission purchased and operated a hotel; a guest at the hotel lost a sum of money through the negligence of a hotel employee who failed to deposit it in the safe. The guest sued the commission for recovery and was met by the defense that it had no authority to operate a hotel and could not be held liable for its *ultra vires* acts. When the case reached the state supreme court, both parties agreed that this was the central issue. The court disposed of it quickly by holding that the commission had power to operate a hotel, and was liable for the restitution of the guest's loss.[9] The analogy between the scope of the commission's activities and those of state park authorities is close, and there are many decisions to the effect that the operation of a hotel is appropriately incidental to the administration of a state or other public park. It may be remembered, too, that colleges and universities may and do frequently operate facilities for the accommodation of transient paying guests.

[9] *New Harmony Memorial Commission* v. *Harris,* 219 Ind. 73, 36 N.E. 2d 856 (1941).

CHAPTER XIX
THE TORT RESPONSIBILITY OF
PRIVATELY CONTROLLED INSTITUTIONS

THE tendency toward softening the harsh rule of charitable immunity from tort responsibility shows a gradual acceleration. A landmark of the period was the publication of the opinion of the United States Court of Appeals for the District of Columbia in its affirmance of the District Court decision in the Georgetown University case of 1940. In this instance Mr. Justice Wiley Rutledge produced an exhaustive and scholarly dissertation thoroughly reviewing the history and present state of this branch of law, and trenchantly pointing to a cogent conclusion.

In Federal Courts

The District Court decision holding Georgetown University liable to a special nurse who was injured by the negligence of one of its own student nurses, on the ground that the special nurse was not an employee of the university and was therefore a "stranger to the charity," was digested in the predecessor to this volume (*The Colleges and the Courts*, 1936–40, p. 93). Justice Rutledge approved the District Court decision, but not on the narrow "stranger to the charity" theory. Instead he believed the conclusion should stand on the broader ground that there is no sound or necessary reason for any charitable immunity.

Justices Miller and Edgerton concurred fully, but Justices Stephens and Vincent and Chief Justice Groner favored affirmance of the judgment of the lower court without broadening the basis of decision, though they filed no separate opinions.

Summarizing his comprehensive study of the decisions from all jurisdictions, Justice Rutledge wrote:

> Paradoxes of principle, fictional assumptions of fact and consequence, and confused results characterize judicial disposition of these claims. From full immunity, through varied but inconsistent qualifications to general responsibility is the gamut of decision.

Concluding that charitable immunity should be abolished, he was not unmindful that the principle of insurance can be utilized

to guarantee indemnity to innocent aggrieved parties and protect charitable institutions from any dire consequences:[1]

> Insurance must be carried to guard against liability to strangers. Adding
> beneficiaries cannot greatly increase the risk of the premium. This
> slight additional expense cannot have the consequences so frequently
> feared in judicial circles, but so little realized in experience. To offset
> the expense will be the gains of eliminating another area of what has
> been called 'protected negligence' and the anomaly that the institutional
> doer of good asks exemption from responsibility for its wrong, though
> all others must pay. The incorporated charity should respond as do pri-
> vate individuals, business corporations and others, when it does good in
> the wrong way.

Other recent cases show that inroads are being made upon
the former immunity of privately controlled nonprofit educational institutions from tort liability. At Brigham Young University a freshman girl was injured by an explosion in the laboratory when she and her two fellow workers made a mistake in
performing an assigned experiment in chemistry. The testimony showed that the instructor had left the room while the
three girls were working on the experiment, and a jury found
him negligent and the federal District Court awarded the injured girl a judgment against the university. The United States
Circuit Court of Appeals, in affirming the judgment, made a
significant statement:[2]

> In our opinion the supreme court of Utah, after much difficulty and
> contrariety of opinion, has definitely and conclusively for the present re-
> pudiated the doctrine of immunity generally accorded charitable institu-
> tions not operating for profit, especially if the tort be against a paid
> patient, or, as in this instance, a student.

Circuit Judge Phillips dissented, taking a conservative view
and arguing that the instructor's negligence, if any, was not the
proximate cause of the injury, and that the cost and value of the
educational services rendered by the university are so greatly in
excess of the tuition charges that it ought to be regarded as a
charity immune from liability for the negligence of its employees.

---

[1] *President and Directors of Georgetown College* v. *Hughes*, (U.S.C.A. for D.C.), 130 F.
2d 810 (1942), affirming *Same*, (U.S.D.C.), 33 F. Supp. 867 (1940).

[2] *Brigham Young University* v. *Lillywhite*, (U.S.C.C.A.), 118 Fed. 2d 836, 137 A.L.R.
598 (1941). Certiorari denied, 314 U.S. 638, 62 S. Ct. 73, 86 L. Ed. 512 (1941).

CONNECTICUT AND OHIO

At Yale University an alumnus of the Class of 1899 attended the fortieth anniversary reunion of his class, and joined other alumni in the old Wolf's Head house from 12 midnight to 2 A.M., when all left the building but lingered briefly on the approaches. After a few minutes this alumnus felt an immediate necessity to urinate, and, noticing that the building was closed and dark, he walked toward what he thought was a bush on the lawn, but was in fact the top of a tree growing from a level ten and one-half feet below and slightly beyond a retaining wall whose parapet extended only some ten to eleven inches above the lawn. He fell over the parapet and down to the lower level, sustaining serious injuries. Testimony was to the effect that the region was "generally well-lighted at the time," but at the trial of the damage suit the jury inspected the premises and returned a verdict for the plaintiff, and judgment thereon was entered against the university. On appeal the judgment was affirmed on the theory that the plaintiff was an invitee on the premises and reasonable care was not exercised by the university because photographs convinced the court that the spot was a trap, dangerous to life and limb. The question of contributory negligence, and that of an invitee who exceeds the limits of his invitation, were argued but not considered pertinent to the facts in this case.[3]

Readiness to hold a charitable corporation responsible for its torts, at least when coupled with lack of care in assigning an employee, was exhibited by the supreme court of Ohio, where two children were injured at the zoological park maintained by the Cleveland Museum of Natural History. For the amusement and edification of visitors, the zoo offered short rides in a howdah on the back of Osa, the elephant. Although the zoo had in its employ an experienced elephant handler, it allowed these rides to be conducted by a keeper who knew little about elephants, and was equipped only with an elephant-hook not in good condition for the purpose. On the day of the accident, one of the passengers on one of the rides was a lady who, shortly after beginning the ride, demanded and was permitted to dismount immediately, saying she knew elephants very well and

[3] *Guilford* v. *Yale University et al.*, 128 Conn. 449, 23 A. 2d 917 (1942).

there was something wrong with Osa. The plaintiff children were thereupon put aboard. Osa suddenly tired of the whole business and bolted for the elephant-house, scraping off howdah and children unceremoniously as she entered the door, thus causing the injuries.

In the trial court verdicts and judgments for each of the plaintiffs were had, but these were reversed by the Court of Appeals. In turn the Ohio supreme court reversed the Court of Appeals and affirmed the judgments of the trial court, on the theory that the verdicts were not against the weight of the evidence, and even though the owner of the elephant was a charitable institution, it was liable for lack of ordinary care in assigning an employee to handle and control the animal.[4]

NEW YORK AND CALIFORNIA

Syracuse University was sued for damages by a woman who attended a football game in Archbold Stadium in November 1937, and who, while tendering her ticket at the gate, was knocked down and trampled by a group of disorderly persons who "rushed the gate." She charged that the university was negligent in having failed to make adequate provision to control the size and type of crowd which was reasonably to have been anticipated. She lost her case in the appellate division by the narrow vote of three judges against two, and the decision was affirmed by the New York Court of Appeals.[5]

When New York University was sued by a student who alleged he was injured by reason of defective instructional equipment and failure of the university to provide proper safeguards, the university answered that it was a charitable institution, and that the negligence, if any, was of the professor in charge. The trial court held this answer insufficient in law; and the Appellate Division approved this ruling and dismissed an appeal.[6] This meant, of course, that the doctrine of charitable immunity is not a complete defense in New York, and that the university must make further answer or lose by default.

A similar outcome appeared in California, where a student at

---

[4] *Newman* v. *Cleveland Museum of Natural History*, 143 Ohio St. 369, 55 N.E. 2d 575 (1944).

[5] *Lowery* v. *Syracuse University*, 282 N.Y. 793, 27 N.E. 2d 203 (1940).

[6] *Weltman* v. *New York University*, 264 App. Div. 907, 35 N.Y.S. 2d 892 (1942).

Stanford University was seriously hurt while participating in the annual "clean-up day" at a Convalescent Home on the campus, in accord with university custom. Riding in the rear part of a pick-up truck on the way back to the academic campus, through a portion of the extensive university lands along San Francisquito Creek, he was shot in the eye with a "BB gun" by an unknown boy along the road, causing loss of the eye. In the trial court he was met with a judgment of nonsuit; but the Court of Appeal reversed the judgment and held that the question of whether the university exercised due care in keeping its grounds safe should have gone to the jury. In this instance the court was impressed by testimony in the record that although the 9,000-acre campus was a game refuge and hunting was forbidden, the use of BB guns and small rifles by boys in the vicinity where the injury occurred was known to have been promiscuous for two years or more. This seemed to raise serious question as to the efficiency of the campus policing; and it was disclosed that when the injury occurred only one campus policeman was on duty.[7] After the facts were put to the jury in the trial court, however, the result was a verdict in favor of the university.

TEXAS AND MICHIGAN

Southern Methodist University at Dallas was sued for injuries sustained by a woman patron at a football game where temporary bleachers collapsed. On her behalf it was alleged that the bleachers were overcrowded beyond their capacity, and that they were faultily constructed of materials which had been allowed to become old, weakened, and defective. A further allegation that the university employee who managed the bleachers was incompetent was at first a part of the pleadings, but was withdrawn early in the proceedings. The trial court directed a verdict for the university and entered judgment accordingly, holding (1) that negligence had not been proved, and (2) that the university was immune as a charitable corporation.

The Court of Civil Appeals reversed and remanded the decision, directing that the question of negligence must be put to the jury. "In Texas," said this court, "a charitable institution's

---

[7] *Stockwell* v. *Board of Trustees of Leland Stanford Junior University*, 64 Cal. App. 2d 197, 148 P. 2d 405 (1944).

responsibility in tort is measured by the relationship existing toward the injured party. To those directly receiving benefits, such as a hospital patient, university student, or other direct recipient, the liability is only for want of ordinary care in the selection of employees or servants. To others not thus directly benefited, such as invitees, strangers, or its own employees, liability is wholly governed by the rule of *respondeat superior*. . . ." The paying visitor at the football game was in this latter category; and this intermediate court asserted the unqualified doctrine that "Charitable institutions are on the same basis as other corporations and individuals as to liability for negligence to those who are non-beneficiaries."

But no, said the Texas supreme court when the case came up on appeal. Conceding only that "It seems definitely established in this state that a charity corporation is liable to an employee for injuries proximately caused by the negligence of its officers, vice principals, or agents," the supreme court denied that the principle applied to invitees or strangers on the premises. Retreating to the classic theory of immunity on grounds of public policy, it expounded the well-known argument that funds dedicated to a public charitable purpose must not be diverted to compensate for a mere private grievance; and reiterated that the injured party has recourse against the individual responsible for the injury. If this individual is insolvent, too bad; but "the courts can not undertake to provide a solvent defendant for every wrong done." Thus the trial court judgment absolving the university was affirmed by the highest Texas court.[8]

The same conclusion was reached in a subsequent case involving the Rice Institute at Houston, where a girl spectator at a football game in Rice Stadium caught the high heel of her shoe in the crack between the planks of the platform near her seat, so that she fell and received severe injuries. The jury returned a verdict for $20,000 damages to the girl and $500 to her father, but the trial court rendered judgment for the defendant Institute notwithstanding the verdict, and this judgment was affirmed by the Court of Civil Appeals, expressly following the precedent set by the supreme court.[9]

---

[8] *Southern Methodist University* v. *Clayton*, 142 Tex. 179, 176 S.W. 2d 749 (1944), reversing (Tex. Civ. App.), 172 S.W. 2d 197 (1943).

[9] *Scott et al.* v. *William M. Rice Institute*, (Tex. Civ. App.), 178 S.W. 2d 156 (1944).

A more recent Texas decision is of much less significance. Here a charitable corporation "on paper" was found to be operating a boarding and rooming house for profit as its sole activity and was held responsible in tort for causing the loss of an article of personal property belonging to a woman lodger.[10]

Edison Institute is the corporate name of the philanthropic undertaking through which Henry Ford maintains an extensive museum of early American history. It is a nonprofit corporation "to demonstrate, for educational purposes, the development of American arts, sciences, customs and institutions by reproducing or reenacting the conditions and circumstances of such development in any manner calculated to convey a realistic picture thereof." The museum, known as Greenfield Village, near Dearborn, Michigan, represented an investment of some $20,000,-000 in land, buildings and equipment. When the present case arose in 1936, the place was open to the public at a fee of 25 cents for adults, and children were admitted free. There was a virtually negligible income from small sales of products made in the museum. Annual operating deficits were personally paid by Henry Ford or members of his family, who were the sole stockholders.

A part of the service to visitors was free transportation in a horse-drawn carriage on the premises. The plaintiff in this case used that service, and as she alighted from the carriage the horses took fright at a violent thunderstorm then in progress, bolted, and caused her to be injured. Her case first went to trial before a jury on the facts alone, and there was a verdict for $1,000 damages. The trial court, upon subsequent proof of the nature of the defendant corporation, rendered judgment in favor of the defendant, *non obstante veredicto*. This judgment, absolving the Institute, was affirmed by the supreme court of Michigan. There was no evidence of negligence in selecting and retaining the driver, the team, or the carriage; and, "The law is well settled in this State that a charitable institution is not liable to a beneficiary for the torts of its servants, unless it was negligent in the selection and retention of the employees and the instrumentalities used by it in carrying on its benevolent purposes."[11] The resemblance to the Texas decision is notable.

[10] *Coefficient Foundation* v. *Edwards*, (Tex. Civ. App.), 188 S.W. 2d 699 (1945).
[11] *De Groot* v. *Edison Institute*, 306 Mich. 339, 10 N.W. 2d 907 (1943).

Where the Tort-Feasor Is Not Acting as Agent or Employee of the Institution

A physician at the Duke University Hospital was employed by the university as professor of obstetrics and gynecology to teach and to do "free ward work" for charity patients, but not to treat paying patients; but he was allowed to receive and treat paying private patients in the office which the university provided for him. One such patient was injured by radium burns allegedly due to negligence of this physician in the course of post-partum treatments, and sued the university for damages. The evidence showed that the university hospital allowed its physicians to carry on private practice as above indicated, but required them to collect their own fees through business organizations of their own. Incoming private patients always got the physician they asked for if they expressed a preference, but if not, assignments were made by a young woman whose salary came from three sources: two private doctors' organizations and the hospital. Thus the university kept as clear as possible from any connection with its physicians' private practice.

Looking at the facts and resolving all doubt in favor of the university, the court affirmed a judgment of nonsuit in this case:

> There was no evidence that Dr. Carter in treating Mrs. Smith assumed to act for Duke University otherwise than in his individual capacity as a practicing physician, or that Dr. Carter was held out by the defendant as having been employed by it to treat pay patients, or that the hospital undertook to furnish physicians and surgeons for the treatment of the maladies of the patients, and hence no liability can attach to the defendant on the theory that Dr. Carter was acting within the scope of an apparent authority or employment.

Having reached that conclusion, the court expressly refrained from deciding the hypothetical question of whether the university is immune from tort responsibility as a charitable institution, provided that it selects its employees with due care.[12]

Workmen's Compensation Act Protects Employees, Not Independent Contractors

A workman was accidentally electrocuted on the campus of Elon College, and an award to his widow of compensation for

[12] *Smith* v. *Duke University*, 219 N.C. 628, 14 S.E. 2d 643 (1941).

his death by the Industrial Commission of North Carolina was affirmed by the trial court, but reversed by the state supreme court because it appeared that he was not an employee of the college. The college maintained its own electrical transmission system and bought its electricity wholesale from the Duke Power Company. The campus system needed repairs consisting of the setting of some new poles and the transfer of the wires to them. In a conversation between the business manager of the college and a local employee of the power company it was suggested that some electricians employed by the company would like to do the work in off hours, and an understanding was had that the college would pay $30 for the job. The college had its own regular employees dig six holes, and obtained the poles to be set in them. Later three linemen presented themselves after hours and were shown the layout, and they set to work after it was agreed that they could borrow from the college some shovels and a saw, and the use of a truck to "back in" the poles, and have the help of some Negro employees of the college at necessary moments. One of the linemen told the business manager that some trees near the new line would have to be trimmed, and the business manager said he would prefer not to have the trees trimmed, and would rather cut ten feet off the poles. This was agreed.

After the fatal accident the other linemen eventually procured a substitute for the deceased, and completed the job. The court's finding that the deceased never was in the employ of the college was based on the fact that the college did not select him, or stipulate the hours or the days on which he should work, or prescribe any detailed method of doing the work, or allocate to him any specific portion of the $30 for the job. It could not have discharged him without breaking the entire job contract. Under these circumstances, thought the court, the linemen were independent contractors and not employees of the college, and hence not under the protection of the workmen's compensation act. The decision was difficult, with three of the justices dissenting.[13]

An Action Based on Alleged Fraud

A very unusual case arose in California, where a woman plaintiff sued as joint defendants the Stanford University Hospital,

[13] *Hayes v. Board of Trustees of Elon College*, 224 N.C. 11, 29 S.E. 2d 137 (1944).

Lane Hospital, the Cutter Laboratory (a corporation), the Board of Trustees of Stanford University as a corporation and as individuals, and two other named persons. She alleged that the defendants manufactured and distributed a compound known as dinitrophenol, and knowingly made false statements and representations that it was harmless, when in fact it was a dangerous drug and likely to cause blindness. In an effort to cure obesity, she took the drug from March to December 1934 as prescribed by her physician, and as a result lost the sight of both eyes. In the trial court her suit was dismissed on demurrer on account of a defect in the pleadings, and after much delay an amended complaint based on alleged fraud instead of negligence was also defeated by demurrer and this conclusion sustained by the Court of Appeal in 1941. In 1942, however, the decision was reversed, as against the contention that the changed basis of the plea constituted an abandonment of the original action and the institution of a new action, which would have been barred by the statute of limitations. Thus the courts were open to further proceedings. The case is important chiefly because it indicates the establishment of a precedent in California to the effect that technical procedural errors and delays will not of themselves be allowed to extinguish the rights of an aggrieved party.[14] Ultimately the case was compromised out of court.

[14] *Wennerholm et al.* v. *Stanford University School of Medicine et al.*, 20 Cal. 2d 713, 128 P. 2d 522, 141 A.L.R. 1358 (1942), reversing *Same*, (Cal. App.), 113 P. 2d 736 (1941).

CHAPTER XX
INSTITUTIONAL REAL PROPERTY

THE acquisition and alienation of real estate, and the erection of college and university buildings, including methods of financing and transactions with building contractors, produced the following cases.

ACQUISITION BY ESCHEAT

North Carolina has long had a statute making the state university the beneficiary of the estates of persons who die intestate and without heirs-at-law. In 1931 a girl died intestate at the age of eighteen, unmarried and childless, being the illegitimate daughter of a predeceased mother. Her lands passed to the state and the university, and were subsequently acquired by a county board of education in 1937. Her mother's sister then claimed the lands as a collateral heir, and was made defendant in an action of ejectment. It was found that her claim could not prevail because up to 1935 collateral heirs could not inherit by operation of law from the estate of an illegitimate child. A statute of 1935 removed this disability, and if the death had occurred thereafter the result would have been different. Under the facts of this case, title was held to have vested in the university without the necessity of judicial determination.[1]

QUITCLAIM DEED BY MORTGAGOR DOES NOT EXTINGUISH THE MORTGAGE LIEN

In North Dakota the State Board of University and School Lands made a loan of $800 to one Augustadt, taking a first mortgage on his farm. Taxes on the farm became delinquent in 1931, and Sheridan County bought the place at tax sale in 1932. There was no redemption, and a tax deed was issued to the county in 1940. The interest on the loan was also delinquent, and in 1941 the Board of University and School Lands took a quitclaim deed to the place, under a statute of 1935 which authorized this procedure in lieu of foreclosure. Question then arose as to the rights of the state and the county. The court held that the county was owner of the land, subject to the lien of the state's

[1] *Board of Education of Chowan County* v. *Johnston*, 224 N.C. 86, 29 S.E. 2d 126 (1944).

first mortgage. The quitclaim deed did not cut off the county's rights nor extinguish the state's mortgage lien. Therefore the county was the owner, and it could elect to pay the mortgage debt, or redeem after foreclosure, or sell to a purchaser who would take the same rights.[2]

Alienation of Unused Part of Campus

Huntingdon College, a denominational college for women in Montgomery, Alabama, received by deed of trust in 1907 a parcel of 58 acres of land to be used "as a place for the education of white women, under the auspices of the Alabama Methodist Conferences." The deed expressly provided that the property should never revert to the grantors or their heirs. Many years later the city of Montgomery extended Bankhead Avenue in such manner as to cut off the western one-third of the tract. This remnant of land was never used for college purposes, and the college determined to sell it and apply the proceeds toward payment of a debt of $129,000 which stood against the $900,-000 college plant. A declaratory judgment authorizing the sale was granted, on the theory of *cy pres* or "equitable approxima-tion," whereby it was decided that changed conditions made the sale of the land the best way to apply it to the general charitable purpose for which it was held in trust. The Alabama statute cov-ering this subject stipulates that any possible reversioners must be made parties in such a case; but that clause was not applicable here, because the original deed expressly negated reversion.[3]

Alleged Conveyance in Fraud of Creditors

Blue Ridge College was incorporated at New Windsor, Mary-land, in 1910, on the initiative of a church corporation entitled the Eastern Maryland District Meeting of the Church of the Brethren, as an institution for students and teachers of that de-nomination. The college was a stock corporation with one thou-sand shares of $25 par value.

In 1937 the church owned 940 shares of the stock. The col-lege had a 25-acre campus and buildings, 275 acres of farm land devised to it in 1933, and a small special endowment be-

---

2 *State v. Sheridan County*, 72 N.D. 254, 6 N.W. 2d 51 (1942).
3 *Heustess v. Huntingdon College et al.*, 242 Ala. 272, 5 So. 2d 777 (1942).

queathed by the same donor. It had subscriptions to general endowment aggregating $86,000, all on condition that if the college ceased to be operated under the control of the church, the endowment would become the property of the General Education Board of the church. Only about $30,000 of the subscriptions had been collected, and this had all been invested in buildings on the campus, secured by notes from the college to the endowment fund. The college also owed the Alumni Association Account some $3,000, and was indebted to various other creditors about $15,000.

A purchaser referred to as "New Jersey interests" wished to buy the campus and buildings and all the capital stock of Blue Ridge College, with intent to operate it as a nonsectarian private institution. The church corporation and the college board of trustees decided to sell, thus closing the career of the college as a denominational institution. The transaction was accomplished as follows: Blue Ridge College conveyed by deed to the church corporation all its holdings except the campus and buildings, and executed to the church corporation a mortgage on the campus and buildings. In return the church transferred to the college its 940 shares of the capital stock, and assumed the debts of the college, including $5,000 commission to the agent who negotiated the sale. The evidence showed that no creditor objected to the transaction, and that all notes previously given by Blue Ridge College were thereafter promptly paid or renewed by the church as they matured.

The new owners of the college took possession of the campus and buildings in 1937, but their enterprise proved to be not financially successful. Later a suit was brought by persons who had become creditors subsequent to the sale of 1937, including four teachers claiming salaries for the years 1940–41 and 1941–42, asking to have the deed and mortgage to the church declared void as having been executed with intent to defraud creditors of the college. In fact these persons were not creditors of the defunct Blue Ridge College, but of its successor, by whatever name. The only color of a claim against the church arose from the circumstance that it, no longer owning or operating any college at the site of Blue Ridge College, yet was a disinterested holder of a mortgage on the campus and buildings operated by the successor institution. There was no evidence of fraudulent intent, and an erroneous judgment of the trial court nullifying the deed and mortgage, apparently based on a misconception of the relations of the parties, was reversed and the case dismissed by the Maryland Court of Appeals, with five justices sitting and all concurring.[4]

The "Special Fund Doctrine"; Validating State University Bonds for Dormitory Construction

A principle already well-established in recent years was affirmed anew in Oklahoma in 1945 when the regents of the state university asked judicial approval of a $275,000 issue of "Apartment Dormitory Bonds" issued and sold under authority of a statute approved March 2, 1945, stipulating that "the bonds issued hereunder shall not be an indebtedness of the State of Oklahoma or of the institution for which they are issued or the Board of Regents thereof, but shall be special obligations payable solely out of the revenues to be derived from the operation of the building. . . ." A similar recital appeared on the face of the bonds. The supreme court, taking original jurisdiction of the matter, readily declared that the statute and the transaction were entirely unaffected by the constitutional limitation of indebtedness of state agencies, and granted an order approving the bonds.[5]

Liability of Surety on Building Contract

A Kentucky case furnishes an indication that the courts are not inclined to allow the surety for a defaulting contractor to interpose purely technical defenses and thus escape responsibility. The Eastern Kentucky State Teachers College engaged a heating company to do $16,000 worth of plumbing in connection with a new swimming pool. The company sublet certain portions of the work, but before it was completed abandoned the contract and filed a petition in bankruptcy, after making an affidavit that all bills for material and labor had been paid. In fact some $6,000 in valid claims were outstanding at that time. The college paid the heating company a total of about $11,-000 on the contract prior to its abandonment.

4 *Eastern Maryland District Meeting of Church of Brethren* v. *Union Bridge Banking and Trust Co. et al.,* (Md.), 40 A. 2d 518 (1945).

5 *Application of Board of Regents of University of Oklahoma,* 195 Okla. 641, 161 P. 2d 447 (1945).

The college then employed another company to complete the work for about $4,000, thus saving about $1,000 on the original contract price, and credited the saving on its claims against the bankrupt. Meantime the subcontractors completed their work at the request of the college and took the necessary steps to perfect their liens. The college then sued the surety for the bankrupt, on the bond guaranteeing faithful performance of the contract. Although the bond was not technically so drawn as to make the surety conclusively liable for the payment of subcontractors, yet the court, with an eye for the requirements of justice, brushed aside this and other highly technical defenses, and awarded the college a judgment for the amount in dispute.[6]

ILLICIT "KICKBACKS" PAID BY BUILDING CONTRACTORS TO UNIVERSITY SUPERINTENDENT OF BUILDING

Another facet of the unsavory situation prevailing at Louisiana State University prior to 1939 came to light in the federal income tax case of one Caldwell, who was employed by the university as superintendent of building operations. The case concerned his personal income for the years 1935–38 inclusive. During those years his salary ranged from $4,500 to $6,000, but in 1936 President J. M. Smith agreed to pay him in addition one per cent of the cost of buildings erected under his supervision, and in 1938 this additional compensation was raised to two per cent, the justification being that the supervision of construction being done by 700 to 800 WPA workers, many of whom were unskilled, was extraordinarily difficult. The United States Board of Tax Appeals held this additional income taxable, but this part of the decision was reversed by the Circuit Court of Appeals, deciding that the transaction was not a "practical embezzlement" of public funds, and that it was exempt under the act of Congress of 1939 prohibiting taxation as income for years prior to 1939 of "compensation for personal service as an officer or employee of a State, or any agency or instrumentality thereof," unless pursuant to an assessment made prior to January 1, 1939, and abating assessments later made. It was noted that both Smith and Caldwell were in the penitentiary at the time of the trial, and did not testify.

6 *Fidelity and Casualty Co. of New York* v. *Board of Regents of Eastern Kentucky State Normal School and Teachers College*, 287 Ky. 439, 152 S.W. 2d 581 (1941).

As to sums shown to have been paid to Caldwell by building contractors as "kickbacks," the judgment of the Board of Tax Appeals was affirmed. "It may be that they were in some cases a fraud on the State for which it may recover, and that Caldwell may become entitled in the year of such payment to a deduction; but until then they are his income." Computation of his income tax in accord with these conclusions was ordered, and the assessment of a fraud penalty against him was held to have been warranted.[7]

Collective Bargaining with Building Service Employees Under State Labor Relations Act

In a controversy with building service employees working in the building at 1680 Broadway, New York City, owned by Columbia University and managed on a commission basis by its agent, the Bethlehem Engineering Corporation, the university and its agent were ordered by the New York State Labor Relations Board to bargain collectively with Local B–32, Building Service Employees' Union, of the American Federation of Labor. The order was affirmed by the trial court, but reversed by the Appellate Division, and the reversal affirmed by the New York Court of Appeals. It was conceded that the building service workers were employees of the university; and the university relied on Section 715 of the state Labor Relations Act, which exempted charitable, educational, or religious associations or corporations from its provisions. The trial court proceeded on the theory that the exemption applied only to employees of the university actually engaged in the discharge of its functions as an educational institution; but the higher courts held that the test is solely the character of the employer, and not the nature of the activity.[8]

---

[7] *Caldwell* v. *Collector of Internal Revenue*, (U.S.C.C.A.), 135 F. 2d 488 (1943).
[8] *Trustees of Columbia University in the City of New York* v. *Herzog*, 269 App. Div. 24, 53 N.Y.S. 2d 617 (1945), reversing *Same*, 181 Misc. 903, 46 N.Y.S. 2d 130 (1944). Affirmed, 295 N.Y. 605, 64 N.E. 2d 351 (1945).

CHAPTER XXI
ACCESSORY EDUCATIONAL CORPORATIONS AND ASSOCIATIONS

IT seems that most of the cases of 1941–45 in this category relate to the tax exemption of fraternity houses and other university facilities in the hands of private nonprofit corporations.

TAXABILITY OF STATE UNIVERSITY BUILDINGS TECHNICALLY OWNED BY PRIVATE CORPORATION

The University of Illinois Foundation was created to hold title to several self-liquidating buildings on the campus and stand as debtor until their cost is amortized. This device enables such buildings to be financed without any suggestion of pledging the credit of the state. It accomplishes essentially the same result as is reached in many other states by the enactment of statutes authorizing the university to issue credit instruments payable solely out of the income to be derived from the operation of the buildings which the borrowed funds are used to erect and equip. Compare the case of the University of Oklahoma in Chapter XX, immediately preceding. The University of Illinois Foundation also has the function of encouraging and receiving gifts for educational purposes at the university.

The county tax collector assessed for the year 1942 four buildings to which the Foundation held title: the Student Union Building, erected with the aid of a long-term federal loan; three men's residence halls with an aggregate capacity of 900 students, erected on a self-liquidating plan without a federal loan; the Illini Building and the Arcade, both of which were acquired in 1941 from the University of Illinois Union, together with mortgage debts, subsequently refinanced. These buildings housed the great variety of accessory services commonly found at a large university, including dormitories, dining halls, restaurants, bowling alleys, barber shop, bookstore, and others. The Illini Building had in the basement the offices and plant of the daily student newspaper. The Arcade contained a cooperative bookstore operated by the university and a barber shop and a restaurant operated by private concessionaires. All these varied services were largely, though not wholly, limited to the patronage of students and faculty members.

Looking at the Foundation solely as an operator in the field of finance and real estate, the tax collector contended that its properties were not properly exempt as devoted to educational uses. The Illinois supreme court declared this argument untenable:

> Whatever income may be derived from the four buildings here is used to promote, and is incidental to, the primary purpose, namely, to provide adequate facilities for university purposes,—in short, 'a public educational purpose.'

Therefore the trial court judgment in favor of the Foundation was affirmed. It was not thought necessary to discuss the matter of whether the buildings were in reality owned by the state of Illinois. Evidently irked by the arguments in behalf of the collector, the court added a peroration emphasizing that the presence of the university greatly enhances the value of other property in the local community. "The University brings many benefits, and this factor is one underlying the exempt character of its property. These facts should be apparent to taxing officers, as well as to other persons."[1]

Taxation of Fraternity Property

The taxation of fraternity houses was litigated in three states with diverse results. A corporation owning the Chi Omega sorority house at the University of Georgia sought an injunction to restrain the collection of taxes, on the ground that its charter described it as "an institution of purely public charity" and stipulated that no private person may ever have any right or interest in its property, all of which must be used to advance education. The supreme court of Georgia, affirming the refusal of an injunction and holding the property taxable, remarked that the crucial test is the actual use of the property and not the words of the charter of the corporation owning it. Stressing the fact that all members of the sorority paid substantial fees for initiation and local and national dues, in addition to a standard price for room and board, one-third of which went to the corpora-

[1] *People ex rel. Goodman, County Collector,* v. *University of Illinois Foundation et al.,* 388 Ill. 363, 58 N.E. 2d 33, 157 A.L.R. 851 (1944).

tion as rentals, the court said, "We do not find that the corporation has provided a home for young women unable to pay board," and thus dismissed its claim to be regarded as a charitable institution.[2]

A tortuous course of legislation and litigation in New Jersey produced a short period in the late 'thirties and early 'forties during which fraternity houses were exempt, but such property has been subject to local taxation since 1942. In *The Colleges and the Courts*, 1936–40, at page 111, we noticed that in the case of *Alpha Rho Alumni Association* v. *City of New Brunswick* the court made fraternity property exempt by declaring unconstitutional and void a statute of 1937 which amended the law exempting property of lodges and fraternal orders, by prohibiting the exemption of property of college clubs and fraternities. The decision was not unanimous, but the reasoning of the majority was followed and approved by the supreme court in several companion cases brought by other fraternities at Rutgers, and all the judgments were subsequently affirmed by the Court of Errors and Appeals in memorandum decisions.[3] Thus college fraternities continued exempt by virtue of the statute exempting lodges and similar fraternal organizations.

A 1942 decision was to the same effect, granting exemption at the petition of certain other Rutgers fraternities for the years 1939 and 1940. The words of the Board of Tax Appeals were clear:[4]

> All that is necessary, under the *Alpha Rho* case, is that there be literal compliance with the statute, *i.e.*, that the property be devoted to the uses of a fraternal organization or lodge, any fraternal organization of whatever character, so long as no part of the property is used for profit. This being shown to be so in the present cases, each of these properties must be adjudged exempt for the years here under appeal.

The situation was radically altered late in 1942, however, when in another suit the entire statute exempting lodges and

---

[2] *Mu Beta Chapter, Chi Omega House Corporation* v. *Davison*, 192 Ga. 124, 14 S.E. 2d 744 (1941).

[3] Cases of several fraternities against the city of New Brunswick, 127 N.J.L. 234, 21 A. 2d 732, 127 N.J.L. 231, 21 A. 2d 734, 127 N.J.L. 232, 233, 21 A. 2d 737, 127 N.J.L. 230, 21 A. 2d 739 (1941).

[4] *Alumni Association of Delta Chapter of Zeta Psi Fraternity et al.*, v. *City of New Brunswick*, 20 N.J. Misc. 275, 26 A. 2d 556 (1942).

fraternal orders was declared unconstitutional and invalid.[5] Subsequently college fraternity houses have been subject to local taxation.

TAXATION OF FRATERNITY HOUSES OWNED BY UNIVERSITY

In New York it was held that two fraternity houses on the campus at Cornell University were taxable, though technically owned by the university, having been built under an agreement whereby the fraternities furnished the money and the university bound itself not to evict them without paying the market value of the houses. The fraternities contracted to pay the taxes in the event any taxes should be assessed and collected. Under New York statutes, said the court, the test of exemption is exclusive ownership and exclusive use for educational purposes, and these must coincide. The university's ownership of these houses, it was thought, is severely limited, though technically the fraternities have no lien; but the case was decided chiefly on the court's conclusion that fraternity houses are used for purposes distinctly "social" as well as educational—that their lodgers are chosen on a "social basis"—and their use is therefore not exclusively educational.[6]

> We hold that these buildings are, and are used as private fraternity houses owned by the respective fraternities, either on or off the campus, which are not exempt. Controlling is the fact that the buildings in question are not used exclusively for educational purposes, any more than a fraternity house off the campus.

In Georgia a similar result was reached in a slightly earlier decision, but by different reasoning, and not without a substantial minority dissent. Here the University of Georgia leased a part of the campus to the Sigma Nu Fraternity Home Association for one year with option of successive renewals to an aggregate of 99 years, for one dollar a year, obligating the fraternity group to build a house costing between $20,000 and $35,000, with no right to convey its interest except to sell to some other fraternity at the university. At the termination of the lease the house would become the property of the Regents of the University System of Georgia, who also agreed to provide 60 per cent

[5] *Rutgers Chapter of Delta Upsilon Fraternity* v. *City of New Brunswick et al.*, 129 N.J.L. 238, 28 A. 2d 759 (1942); affirmed, *Same*, 130 N.J.L. 216, 32 A. 2d 364 (1943).
[6] *Cornell University* v. *Thorne*, 184 Misc. 630, 57 N.Y.S. 2d 6 (1945).

of the cost of the house in the form of a 4½ per cent loan, to be amortized in twenty years.

Did this create the relationship of landlord and tenant between the university and the fraternity association, or did it give the latter an "estate for years" for the duration of which the property would be taxable against the fraternity? The majority of the court decided for the second alternative, and held the property subject to levy and sale under tax execution.[7] The two dissenting justices thought the fraternity group ought to be regarded as no more than a tenant, because the 99-year lease was actually a succession of 1-year leases at option, and because of the very limited right of conveyance. "There would be a public sale at which the public could not bid or buy." They thought, in fact, that the fraternity had no transferable interest in the land, and believed the real purpose of the agreement was to make doubly sure that the land would remain in the ownership and control of the Regents. The purely nominal rental, the requirement that a house be built, and various stipulations regarding conformance with university regulations all lent color to this view.

Tort Liability of Fraternity Club as Owner of House

At the University of Minnesota the house of a fraternity chapter was destroyed by fire at night. One of the members was killed and two were seriously injured. One of the injured members sued for damages against the fraternity club holding title to the house, and obtained a verdict and judgment for $6,000 in the trial court, and this was affirmed by the state supreme court. It appeared that a dozen boys slept in a dormitory on the third floor of the house having only a single stairway, and it was not possible for all to escape by the stairway at the time of the fire. One escaped by jumping to a nearby tree, and the plaintiff in this case was injured by dropping from the window to the frozen ground. The issue of negligence turned on whether or not the dormitory had two separate means of egress as required by statute for multiple dwellings. Apparently it had not, and the higher court refused to disturb the findings of the jury on the point.[8] No question of charitable immunity was raised, and prob-

---

[7] *State et al.* v. *Davison*, 198 Ga. 27, 31 S.E. 2d 225 (1944).

[8] *Briggs* v. *Minnesota Delta Upsilon Club*, 212 Minn. 14, 2 N.W. 2d 151 (1942).

ably advisedly. It would be difficult to prove the club charitable, assuming that it desired to make that contention; and even if charitable character were granted, the courts of Minnesota are known to have well-established precedents hostile to the doctrine of charitable immunity.

TABLE OF CASES

TABLE OF CASES

FEDERAL

STATE

ALABAMA

CALIFORNIA

COLORADO

CONNECTICUT

INDEX

INDEX

ALABAMA, University of, 100
American Bible Society, 107
American University, 95, 96
Appropriations, 38–40
Arnold College for Hygiene and Physical Education, 70
Associated Jewish Charities of Baltimore, 100, 101
Atlanta University, 55
Attachment of college funds, 40–41
Attorney general, 40

BAKER University, 90
Barnes Foundation, the, 18, 19
Behnke-Walker Business College, 64
Berea College, 103
Berry School, the, 16
Blue Ridge College, 130, 131
Bonds and other credit instruments, 41–42
Bonnycastle Club, 68
Brigham Young University, xv, 120
Brooklyn College, 20
Buildings, 132–136

CALIFORNIA, University of, xi, 37, 88
Carnegie Endowment for International Peace, 60
Central College, 51, 52
Charleston Library Society, 97, 98
Chi Omega Sorority, 136, 137
Chicago, University of, 45
Cleveland Museum of Natural History, 121, 122
Coefficient Foundation, 125
Collective bargaining, 134
College of the City of New York, 23
Colorado, University of, xi, 37
Colorado Women's College, 94
Columbia University, 5, 77, 78, 105, 134
Congregation of the Holy Cross, 13
Constitutionally independent state universities, xi, 25, 37–38
Consumers' Research, Inc., 70, 71
Contracts
for building construction, 132–133
involving real property, 130–132
of professors and instructors, 18–24
with building service employees, 134
Cornell University, 138

DARTMOUTH College, 103
Daughters of the American Revolution, 101, 102
Debs, Eugene V., 87
Debs Memorial Radio Fund, Inc., 86, 87
Delta Upsilon Fraternity, 138, 139
Douglas, Mr. Justice William O., 79
Drake University, 15
Duke University, 107, 126
Dykstra, Clarence A., 27

EDISON Institute, 125
Elon College, xii, 48, 49, 126, 127
Emory and Henry College, 109
Endowment
investment of in dormitories, 46–47
See also Trust funds, educational
Engineering Society of Detroit, 66
Enoch Pratt Free Library of Baltimore, ix, 6, 7, 8, 45
Escheat, 129
Everson Museum of Art, 99

FACULTY members
compatibility of position with local public office, 26
contracts of, 18–24
discharge of for cause, 19–22
salaries of, 22–25, 28–29
tenure regulations affecting, 19–24
Ford, Henry, 125
Forward Association, 86, 87
Fraternities, 136–139
Funk Seminary, 108

GENERAL Education Board, 105
George, Henry, xiii, 74
Georgetown University, xv, 119
Georgia, Board of Regents of the University System of, xi, 37, 38, 138, 139
Georgia, University of, 136, 137, 138, 139
GI Bill of Rights, 1
Ginn, Edwin, 84
Goucher College, xiv, 46
Governing board, the
right of to employ counsel, 40
Governing board members
compatibility of position with other state office, 34, 35–36
concurrent service of in the army, 34–35
Grenfell Association, the, 78